C000215206

The Toll-houses
of Somerset

Janet Dowding
& Patrick Taylor

POLYSTAR PRESS

ISBN 978 1 907154 05 8

The Toll-houses of Somerset

Published by Polystar Press
277 Cavendish Street
Ipswich Suffolk IP3 8BQ
(01473) 434604
polystar@ntlworld.com

ISBN 978 1 907154 05 8

All rights reserved.
This book is protected by copyright.
No part of it may be reproduced, stored in a
retrieval system, or transmitted, in any form
or by any means, electronic, mechanical,
photocopying, recording or otherwise, without
the written permission of the author or publisher.

Every attempt has been made to trace accurate
ownership of copyrighted material in this book.
Errors and omissions will be corrected in
subsequent editions, provided that
notification is sent to the publisher.

© Janet Dowding & Patrick Taylor 2013

Typeset by nattygrafix

Printed by
R Booth Ltd, The Praze, Penryn

Contents

Illustrations

For
Janet's husband, David Dowding, descendant of Robert Gordon,
Toddington (Glos) 'toll collector'
and
Patrick's aunt, Dora James, descendant of George Hobbs (1789-1864),
Timsbury 'coal miner'

0.0 Introduction

With seven toll-house books already in circulation, this volume is very much an addition to a county series and as the fourth in the west country it follows on from the volumes on Cornwall and Devon. As with the others, the general introductory essay is very much the same, albeit now with local Somerset illustrations. Following this the gazetteer section gives a detailed view of Somerset's toll-houses, including all known sites, illustrated where possible.

This would not have happened without Janet Dowding's enthusiasm and energy for this project; her gazetteer entries, all the more informative for their input from the Census records, fill the second and greater half of the book. There was a temptation to split this volume because of the sheer wealth of material, but the amount proved somewhat less than in the bigger county of Devon, so this has been resisted.

As was stated in the previous volume these books are perhaps a little ahead of their time: when the oil runs out (and rest assured that it will) there will be a wave of nostalgia for this old system of road transport, not dissimilar to that for the railways at the end of the age of steam. The Milestone Society, for which Janet is Somerset representative, is perhaps ahead of the game here, but as the photograph below shows much has already been lost.

Stoberry Toll-gate (re-used on a farm at Bleadney but now destroyed)
photo: Wells Museum

1.0 The Turnpike Roads

Mending the Highways
(from Smith - 1970)

CAP. VIII.
The ftatute for mending of highways.

FOR amending of highways, being now both very noifom and tedious to travel in, and dangerous to all paffengers and carriages :

(2) Be it enacted by the authority of this prefent parliament, that the conftables and church-wardens of every parifh within this realm, fhall yearly upon the *Tuefday* or *Wednefday* in *Eafter* week call together a number of the parifhioners, and fhall then elect and chufe two honeft perfons of the parifh to be furveyors and orderers for one year, or the works for amendment of the highways in their parifh leading to any market-town ; (3) the which perfons fhall have authority by virtue hereof, to order and direct the perfons and carriages that fhall be appointed for thofe works, by their difcretions ; (4) and the faid perfons fo named fhall take upon them the execution of their faid offices, upon pain every of them making default, to forfeit twenty fhillings. *[margin: Who fhall be charged towards the mending of highways. Surveyors fhall be appointed for the amendment of highways. 3 Mod. 96. 22 Car.2.c.12. f. 12.]*

II. And the faid conftables and church-wardens fhall then alfo name and appoint four days for the amending of the faid ways, before the feaft of the nativity of Saint *John Baptift* then next following ; (2) and fhall openly in the church the next *Sunday* after *Eafter* give knowledge of the fame four days ; (3) and upon the faid days the parifhioners fhall endeavour themfelves to the amending of the faid ways ; (4) and fhall be chargeable thereunto as followeth ; that is to fay, every perfon for every plow-land in tillage or pafture that he or fhe fhall occupy in the fame parifh, and every other perfon keeping there a draught or plough, fhall find and fend at every day and place to be appointed for the amending of the ways in that parifh as is aforefaid, one wain or cart furnifhed after the cuftom of the country with oxen, horfes or other cattle, and all other neceffaries meet to carry things convenient for that purpofe, and alfo two able men with the fame, upon pain of every draught making default, ten fhillings ; (5) and every other houfholder, and alfo every cottager and labourer of that parifh, able to labour, and being no hired fervant by the year, fhall by themfelves or one fufficient labourer for every of them, upon every of the faid four days, work and travel in the amendment of the faid highways, upon pain of every perfon making default, to lofe for every day twelve pence. (6) And if the faid carriages of the parifh, or any of them, fhall not be thought needful by the fupervifors to be occupied upon any of the faid days, that then every fuch perfon that fhould have fent any fuch carriage, fhall fend to the faid work for every carriage fo fpared two able men, there to labour for that day, upon pain to lofe for every man fo fent to the faid work, twelve pence. (7) And every perfon and carriage abovefaid fhall have and bring with them fuch fhovels, fpades, picks, mattocks, *[margin: Four days fhall be appointed for the amendment of highways. Six days are appointed by 5 El. c. 13. f. 7. Each perfon's charge towards the mending of highways. Explained by 18 El. c. 10; f. 2. Neceffary tools fhall be brought to be]*

Statute for Mending of Highways, 1555
(from Serjeant & Penrose - 1973)

1.1 The King's Highway

In order to understand the turnpike road system that gave rise to toll-houses in the eighteenth century we need first to look at its origins in the mists of medieval time.

Early roads were not actual parcels of real estate set aside for the purpose of transit as have evolved today, but rather lines of least resistance where a 'right of passage' existed - the King's Highway - over ground that remained in private ownership. This still exists in vestigial form in our modern footpath network, which then as now consisted of three levels of usage: footpaths, bridleways and carriageways (now roads used as public paths). In those days diversions were implemented to maintain the right of the traveller if the road was 'founderous' or his way was blocked, rather than at the request of the owner to suit the management of the land as is now often the case.

The highway was thus a 'communal property right' available freely for the use of any subject of the Crown and as such received little or no maintenance other than out of selfish necessity to overcome a particular obstacle such as a flood or fallen tree. It was therefore in no individual's interest to invest time or money in repairing something that would mainly benefit others.

As a consequence the roads were generally in a very poor state and greatly abused by heavy loads with many horses, by spiked or narrow wheels and by the dragging of sledges or timber. Similar problems exist to this day where the selfish interest of highway users will require legislation to achieve a benefit for the common good (e.g. the limitation of motor car use), and it was indeed legislation then that was a first step on the way to improvement of the situation. A parallel can be seen here with another communal property right, that of the old strip field system with attendant grazing and hunting rights, which was also abused by selfish interest and eventually put to rights by the legislation of the Enclosure Acts.

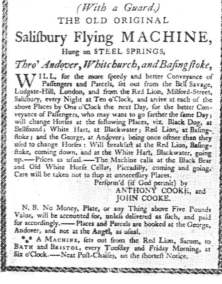

Salisbury Coach Service Poster
(from Wright - 1992)

1.2 Parish Responsibility

In the mid sixteenth century the state of the roads became of such concern that legislation was passed to firmly place the responsibility for their repair in the hands of the parish in which they were situated. The initial Act of 1555, in the brief reign of Mary Tudor, was a temporary measure which required each parish to elect two Surveyors. Their duty was to oversee the repair of roads by the inhabitants of that parish on four days per year when they were to provide 'statute labour'.

The larger landowners were also required to provide two men plus carts and tools whilst the Surveyors were permitted to dig for gravel on any waste land or commons adjoining the road. A further Act of 1562 extended the statute duties to six days per year and defaulters were liable to heavy fines.

Parishes that failed to maintain their roads properly were liable to be presented by the Justices to Quarter Sessions. If they then still failed to repair the roads satisfactorily they would be subject to indictment and the imposition of fines and/or additional days of statute labour. An occasional alternative to this was the raising of a Highway Rate by the Justices, which would then be used to pay for the necessary labour.

The problem which this system failed to tackle was that of the polluter not paying - the major users of the roads in a parish were not the inhabitants, but rather those passing through often with heavy loads for markets in other places. Their contribution to the effort of repair was made in their own parish and was but a fraction in recompense for the wear and tear they inflicted on the roads in general.

The problem of selfish interest therefore remained during a period of increasing trade in the seventeenth century and was not helped by the unwillingness of labourers (one volunteer being worth ten pressed men) nor by Surveyors whose unpaid posts were held on an annual basis and led to low levels of skill and little continuity of effort.

Tarr Steps
Clapper Bridge near Hawkridge
photo: richard raynsford

1.3 Available Technology

At the end of the seventeenth century in archaeological terms, the Iron Age was still very much in progress with timber, fired clay, stone and metal being the major materials for any significant undertaking. Power was sourced from either muscle, wind or water, all three being used in the various forms of mills at fixed locations, the former two for locomotion on land or water. The wonders of steam that could turn heat into motion were as yet unheard of and the nation's wealth was traded and defended by sailing ships of timber, tar and hemp rope.

The transportation of goods thus involved considerable effort and consequently costs away from the cheapest place of production rose sharply. A number of rivers had been made navigable but significant areas remained beyond the reach of water-borne transport. The roads thus acted as both feeders to the river system and as the main means of transport where the rivers did not reach. In addition some goods did not travel well by water, others might not risk military intervention at sea whilst even more were better walking themselves to market. Whilst road transport was many times more expensive per ton per mile, the differential being relatively less for more expensive goods, it was often the preferred alternative.

There was a large network of 'carriers' operating around the country, usually based at various inns and for the most part employing packhorses. The seventeenth century saw these augmented by increasing amounts of wheeled transport, largely as a result of the increasing size and quantity of goods being traded, which led ultimately to a renewed crisis on the roads.

A response to this were the various 'Wheel Acts' which sought to limit the damage to the roads by legislating about permissible loads and wheel widths. These were doomed to failure as, essentially against the spirit of the times, they tried to contain the damage with preventative measures.

> And whereas the Wheels of many Carts, Carrs, and Brewers Drays, now commonly used for the Carriage of Goods, Beer, Ale, and other things, from Place to Place with-in the Cities of London and Westminster, and Parishes aforesaid, where the Streets are Paved, are made thinner or narrower in the Felleys then formerly, and many are Shod with Iron Tyres, by means whereof the Pavements in the Streets of the said Cities and Places are daily impaired and broken up, and made dirty and rough: For preven-tion whereof for the time to come, Be it there-fore Enacted by the Authority aforesaid, That from and after the Fifteenth day of December, the Wheels of every Cart, Carr or Dray to be used for the Carriage of any thing What-soever, from any Place within the said Cities and Places, to any Place situate in the said Cities and Places Where the Streets are Pa-ved, shall be made to contain the full breadth of Six Inches in the Felley, and shall not be wrought about with any Iron Work What-soever, nor be drawn With above the number of two Horses, after they are up the Hills from the Water-side; And the Owners and Pro-

Extract from London Wheel Act, 1690
(from Searle - 1930)

1.4 Justice Trusts

The parish repair system had taken each parish's previous Common Law obligation to maintain local roads and enshrined it in national legislation which was not in fact abolished until the General Highway Act of 1835. The system contained no requirement for the improvement of roads to cater for increased usage and was essentially an evenly applied remedy to a very uneven problem. Considerable differences existed between parishes both in terms of size and the numbers of roads to repair, population density and availability of labour and local geology which affected both the quality of substrate and availability of materials for repair. A further overlay of differing amounts of road usage near towns as trade increased and carriers turned to waggons and coaches led to a result that included many extremes.

In some parishes the roads were doubtless adequate whilst in others they were difficult to start with, poorly repaired and subject to increasingly heavy usage. This final straw was the key to a solution, the earliest tolls levied to pay for repair being those charged by the Justice trusts of the late seventeenth century. The first of these dates from 1663 and was set up to remedy problems on part of the Great North Road, where the Justices had previously tried all else at their disposal without success.

The concept of tolls was not new and had in the past been used to fund both 'pavage' and 'pontage' as well as to recoup costs for occasional private roads. Tolls had also been levied for markets, giving rise to a different type of toll-house in medieval times. It was therefore no great leap to apply such a toll to remedy a problem on a particular public road, the Justices retaining control of both the tolled road and the others within a parish.

A further twelve Justice trusts were set up on particularly bad roads between 1696 and 1714 by which time the turnpike trust proper was beginning to emerge as a more suitable vehicle for setting the roads to rights.

Medieval Bridge at
Bury, near Dulverton
photo: richard raynsford

1.5 Turnpike Trusts

The earliest turnpike trusts date from 1707 and, although still under the control of the Justices who were usually included amongst their number anyway, were run by trustees who were able to spread the administrative load of managing the roads which was threatening to swamp the Justices' other duties. The trusts were composed for the most part of local gentlemen and landowners, who as trustees were not able to profit from the trust itself. They could however foresee the relief afforded to their parishes by the indirect benefits of improved local economies that would ensue from making outsiders pay for the maintenance of the local roads.

Turnpike trusts were but one of many types of local 'ad hoc' body set up during the eighteenth century amongst which are included the Incorporated Guardians of the Poor. These latter set up 'Unions' of several parishes to build a workhouse, which could then be let as a going concern to a local manufacturer who would feed the occupants in return for the use of their labour, thus relieving the parishes of the burden of the poor. These were as much forerunners of local authority Social Services departments as the turnpike trusts were of Highways departments, both marking the beginnings of bringing various systems into public control, without incurring great expense.

It should be remembered that the turnpike trusts were no more than non profit making trusts set up to manage existing routes, very unlike the later canal and railway concerns which were joint stock companies with shareholders whose aim was to create new routes. Each turnpike trust was set up by an Act of Parliament, usually following vigorous petitioning by local worthies about the state of the roads. Parliamentary permission was necessary because the enterprise required the extinction of the former communal right of free passage and it became usual for Acts to last for a period of twenty one years, although renewal was usually forthcoming.

Anno XV.

Caroli II. Regis.

An Act for Repairing

the High-ways within the Counties of *Hertford*, *Cambridge* and *Huntington*.

Whereas the ancient high-way and Post-Road leading from London to York, and fo into Scotland, and likewife from London into Lincolnfhire, lieth for many miles in the Counties of Hertford, Cambridge and Huntington, in many of which places the Road, by reafon of the great and many Loads which are weekly drawn in Waggons throughthe faid places, as well by reafon of the great Trade of Barley and Mault that cometh

Extract from First Turnpike Act, 1663 (from Searle - 1930)

8

1.6 Turnpike Mania

In the years up to 1750 some 133 turnpike trusts received their Acts of Parliament and roads were turnpiked in two main areas. Firstly, and mainly before 1720, the network of radial roads emanating from London were covered by a number of linear trusts, each one's territory abutting the next. This process continued in the following thirty years alongside the second concentration of town-centred trusts which developed along the Severn valley between Bristol (at that time England's second largest city) and a rapidly developing Birmingham.

Around mid-century the turnpike idea seems to have captured the imagination in a big way and between 1751 and 1772 a further 418 Acts were passed, which effectively allowed the turnpike system to cover the country.

The uncertainties that led up to the American War of Independence brought this age of confidence to a sudden halt in 1773 and the ensuing years that also included the Napoleonic Wars saw greatly reduced activity in terms of new trusts. A further 400 or so trusts were set up between 1773 and 1836 of which 59 alone were in the years 1824 to 1826.

These later years of lesser activity were due in part to a saturation point being reached, but should also be seen against the beginnings of the years of the boom in canal building from 1770, along with the industrial revolution getting into full swing doubtless helped along its way by the greatly improved transport, trade and communications links provided by the turnpikes. The final mini-boom in turnpike activity of 1824 to 1826, probably represents a mopping up of the last remaining suitable routes in slightly improved times. Whilst Acts continued to be renewed throughout most of the nineteenth century, the last new Act of 1836 foreshadows the coming of the railways in the 1840's and the growing realisation that the days of the turnpikes were numbered.

Toll-house Lamp, Stoberry
photo: janet dowding

MINEHEAD TURNPIKE.

PREPARATORY to the extinction of this Trust, Messrs. HAWKES and RISDON are instructed to offer for SALE by AUCTION, at the RAILWAY HOTEL, WASHFORD, on THURSDAY, the 27th day of SEPTEMBER instant, at Three o'clock in the afternoon punctually, the undermentioned

TOLL HOUSES,
MATERIALS, AND TOLL GATES, viz.:—

Lots.

1.—The Five Bells toll-house and outbuildings.
2.—The Doniford toll-house and outbuildings.
3.—The Wibble Lane toll-house and outbuildings.
4.—The Alcombe Cross toll-house and outbuildings.
5.—The Timberscombe toll-house and outbuildings.
6.—The materials of the Wheddon Cross toll-house.
7.—The materials of the Green Dragon toll-house.
8.—The materials of the Washford toll-house.
9.—The materials of the Fair Cross toll-house.
10.—The toll-box at Yard Mills.
11.—The Tower-hill toll-house.
12.—The materials of the Stowey toll-house.
13.—The Stowey, Jackson's-lane, and Limekiln-lane toll-gates and posts.
14.—The Putsham toll-gates and posts.
15.—The Wibble-lane toll-gates and posts.
16.—The Doniford toll-gates and posts.
17.—The Watchet west toll-gate and posts.
18.—The Five Bells toll-gates and posts.
19.—The Washford toll-gates and posts.
20.—The Fair Cross toll-bar and posts.
21.—The Yard Mills toll-bar and posts.
22.—The Tower-hill toll-gate and posts.
23.—The Seven Ash toll-bar and posts.
24.—The East Coombe toll-gate and posts.
25.—The Carhampton toll-gates and posts.
26.—The Alcombe Cross toll-gates and posts.
27.—The Dunster toll-gate and posts.
28.—The Timberscombe toll-gate, bar, and posts.
29.—The Wheddon Cross toll-gate, bar, and posts.

Possession to be had on the 1st November next.

All further particulars will be contained in the conditions of sale to be exhibited at the auction, and in the meantime can be obtained on application to either

Mr. THOMAS HAWKES,
Surveyor, Williton,

The Treasurer ; or to

Messrs. WARDEN & PONSFORD,
Solicitors, Bardon, near Taunton,

The Clerks to the Trustees.

Dated 1st September, 1877.

Auction of Assets, 1877
Minehead Turnpike Trust

1.7 Winding Up

By the 1840's the turnpike road system had reached its greatest extent with over 20,000 miles of road under the control of over a thousand trusts. During the preceding century the growth and improvement of the system had greatly reduced travelling times and consequently enlarged the market place. Road construction techniques had gradually improved from the early days of simply piling another layer of gravel on top to the latter years, under the influence of great engineers like Telford or McAdam, when roads were rebuilt with a firm foundation and progressively smaller sized stones rolled in, to provide a freely draining cambered finish.

Inland transportation as a whole, with the complementary system of canals, had been greatly improved but not revolutionised, as it was still essentially bound by the limitations of muscle and wind power. It was the magic of steam in the form of the railways which ultimately brought the revolution. The turnpike system suffered first followed by the canals, as both were swept away as passengers and then freight took to the rails.

The turnpike trusts were thus subjected to falling receipts through the mid-nineteenth century which made it increasingly difficult for them to deliver the goods.

Lack of repairs led to a growing resentment to their charges amongst their customers, perhaps most strongly felt in Wales where the 'Rebecca' Riots of the 1840's saw the destruction of many gates and toll-houses by men curiously disguised in female clothing.

By the 1870's the trusts were being wound up, their assets in the form of toll-houses and equipment were sold off, and the responsibility for the roads, which they still did not own, vested in the Highway Boards, forerunners of the County Councils.

Terminus Stone, Tolland Down
photo: janet dowding

2.0 Collecting the Tolls

Toll Gate Collection
(from Smith - 1970)

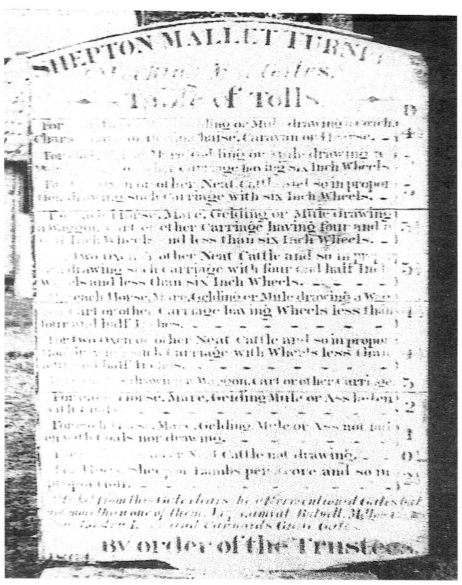

Toll Board from Pecking Mill, 1864
photo from Old Mendip

2.1 Toll Gates & Turnpikes

The turnpike trusts were generally empowered by their Acts of Parliament to 'erect or cause to be erected a gate or gates, turnpike or turnpikes', usually in positions that were left to their own discretion. Certain towns did lobby Parliament and as a result toll-gates could not be placed nearer than three miles distant so as not to discourage local markets. Trusts with linear routes therefore tended to have toll-gates at either end of their territory with occasional others in between, often where a side road joined the way. In contrast the town-centred trusts tended to end up with a ring of toll-gates around the outskirts guarding virtually every road inwards.

The trusts were however compelled to enforce a strictly defined set of toll charges that were to a large degree proportional to the amounts of damage caused by differing types of traffic. Local traffic was often favoured by being allowed a same day return trip at no extra cost and there were a number of common exemptions from toll, notably people going to church or to vote, agricultural traffic, the Army and mail coaches which sounded their horns on approaching the gates.

Most trusts had three main employees: a surveyor to initiate and oversee repairs together with a clerk and treasurer to administer their affairs. Their tasks were to engage labour as required to mend the roads and oversee the collectors employed at each toll-gate. There was an inherent weak link in the system here that depended on the honesty of the collectors or pike-men as they became known. This led in due course to the practice of toll-farming, whereby the proceeds of a toll-gate for the coming year were sold off by auction to 'toll-farmers', either individual collectors with initiative, or contractors who took on themselves the risk of employing several collectors.

The trusts were thus assured of a toll income, which was often supplemented by composition payments from parishes who bought themselves out of their statutory labour obligations.

Burrowbridge Turnpike Gate Ticket
Somerset Industrial Archaeological Society

2.2 Toll-houses

To facilitate the twenty four hour presence of their collectors, the turnpike trusts usually built small associated dwellings at their gates:- the toll-houses. They generally comprised very minimal accommodation of two rooms with a scullery and privy attached, although larger types did become more common in later years. These toll-houses were either one or two storeyed and came in many shapes and sizes, some trusts adopting a standard design whilst others seem to have tried many variations, occasionally even an existing building, if suitably sited, being pressed into service.

If built to a normal rectangular plan they would often have gable windows very close to the front corner of the building or a bay window on the main room to provide the collector with a view up and down the road. A development of the bay came in the form of the octagonal ended house where effectively the bay became the room, this particular form becoming the norm for the toll-house building-type to such an extent that it was also employed at toll collection points on the canals. The octagonal shape also appears in some country house park gatekeeper's lodges, where again an element of control was required.

It may thus have its roots in the neo-classical love of geometry or possibly may be derived from military precedents of a defensive nature, as many toll-houses of the more ornate 'gothick' kind sport the mock battlements of the picturesque. Wherever the shape derived from, it was nevertheless of great utility and maximised the area within the dwellings for a given amount of building material. Much can be said for the presence of the buildings themselves; their many windows and forward position would undoubtedly have unsettled any approaching traveller intent on avoiding the toll with a feeling of having his every move watched. It is this presence that remains today as such a helpful clue to identifying toll-houses, particularly when they are not of the obvious octagonal type.

'Picturesque' Toll-house
Snowdon Hill, Chard
photo: janet dowding

Whilst the pike-man's job required his presence on the premises it was not strictly necessary for him to be on guard looking out of the windows twenty four hours of the day. Most toll-houses were built on very small parcels of land owned by the trustees, usually carved out of the corners of fields, but sufficient to allow the tenants a small cottage garden for their home grown produce. Because of their usual remoteness these small plots often also contained their own well or pump for water supply.

Internally the toll-houses would have been very cramped by modern day standards, particularly if the pike-man had a family of any size. The small bedroom would have slept the whole family, a truckle-bed for the children sliding out from beneath the main one, as can be seen at the Sussex toll-house at the Weald and Downland Museum. The other room served every other purpose, being in every sense the living room, and contained the hearth where food was cooked, together with seating, tables, storage etc. and may well have been awkward to furnish if without any square corners at all. The main door to the highway usually led off this room and it was often protected by a porch or shelter of some kind where the collector could receive tolls in the dry.

Another common indicative feature of toll-houses is a blanked out window at first floor level where a toll-board would have been placed. Sited as they were hard against the highway, those that survive today are perhaps the most visible remains of the turnpike system. The keen industrial archaeologist will also be able to find many examples of contemporary milestones, a later requirement of the turnpike legislation, as most of the roads today that show 'MS' at one mile intervals on Ordnance Survey maps were originally turnpike roads. There are also a few surviving gates, their general form consisting of a main vehicular gate or turnpike (originally a spiked pole) across the road, with usually a pedestrian gate between this and the toll-house.

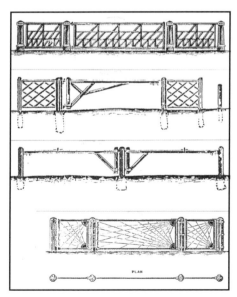

Varieties of Toll Gate
(from Searle - 1930)

2.3 Local Distinctiveness

A particular problem with toll-houses is dating their construction. In between a *terminus post quem* of the original turnpike act and a *terminus ante quem* of finding them on a tithe map or early Ordnance Survey lie many years. Most will be found to have been originally constructed nearer the earlier date at the beginning of a turnpike road's existence and therefore not benefiting from the slightly improved communications that followed by overland transport and even less likely to have benefited from the even greater improvements that the canals later brought to water borne transport.

In terms of their walling materials therefore, toll-houses were almost universally built of what was locally available and remain to this day useful pointers to local distinctiveness and the nature of the geology thereabouts. Thus in Plymouth we find the local Devonian limestone used, in Bath an Oolitic limestone, in Anglesey the local metamorphic rock and at Todmorden, in the Pennines, Millstone Grit. As eighteenth century buildings, where stone was not available, brick was usually the order of the day, so that in Cambridge we find white Gault bricks, whilst in Essex red brick and tile from the London Clay.

Although the timber-frame tradition had long gone into decline, and certainly was less suitable for forming an octagonal building, there is a timber-framed and thatched toll-house in Suffolk, as well as the lap-boarded Sussex example in the Weald and Downland Museum, both of which are rectangular in plan.

Roofing materials show a similar pattern. Thatch was the material of an earlier age and unsuitable anyway as it represented a severe fire risk, should there be any local dissent about the coming of the turnpikes. Pantiles and the larger stone flags and tiles, whilst not best suited to the small areas of hipped roofs involved in octagonal buildings, were sometimes used nevertheless, more so on the rectangular examples.

Red Brick and Tile
Plot Stream, Aller
photo: janet dowding

Slate, however, was the new material of the age and seems to have been the predominant choice, even in the east where it had to be imported from afar. In the eighteenth century roofs were generally pitched according to the materials used, a slate or pantile roof requiring less timber at 30° to 40° pitch, than would a plaintile roof at 45° or more. The presence of a steep slate roof therefore often suggests a replacement covering to an earlier thatch roof.

We have seen that toll-houses were basic small domestic buildings, housing persons fairly low down the social scale. As such they fit within the vernacular tradition, although the tendency has been for them to be studied as curiosities within the province of the industrial archaeologist. Within this vernacular tradition they may be considered somewhere near its later threshold, as particularly with the octagonal forms, there is an overlay of the 'polite', a signalling of their purpose as a particular type of building. This is especially true where a standard design marks their belonging to a particular trust or they venture into the 'picturesque' at the whim of the trustees. The fashionable input could manifest itself as 'gothick' windows or even crenellated parapets, which by this time presumably no longer required the King's licence.

These fashions were however directed from above, being very much the prerogative of the trustees, who as fashionable members of the gentry would have been very aware of the latest ideas and as keen to try them out on their turnpike roads as at their lodge gates. It is therefore possible that the octagonal form used in toll-houses derived from earlier garden buildings of this shape, as is believed to have happened with park lodge gatehouses. The turnpike roads can be seen in this light as a parallel phenomenon to the enclosures and creation of our country house estates. The gentry not only came to control large areas of land, signalling this benign stewardship with their various gatekeeper's lodges, but also the routes between them.

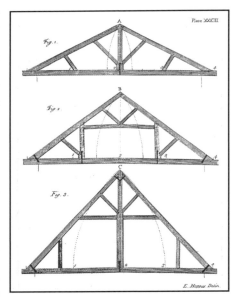

Varieties of Roof Pitch for Different Roofing Materials (from Cruickshank & Wyld - 1975)

2.4 What Lies Ahead?

Local distinctiveness relates to the customs and ways of doing things that have evolved in an area, and which give it a distinctive local character. This 'difference from other places' appears not only in the landscape moulded by our management of the land but also in our built environment. An important part of maintaining local distinctiveness therefore involves celebrating the differences, keeping alive the stories and associations of a place.

The problem with toll-houses in this respect is their situation. They were mostly built in isolation, on the perimeters of our settlements and as a consequence almost never occur within our historic centres, where most modern day celebration of place happens. Whilst the turnpikes probably initiated ribbon development, encouraging the spread of suburban villas, their remains are now largely surrounded by it, so that apart from their intimate link with the actual road, toll-houses have little sense of place.

Unfortunately the road itself has become too fast and dangerous a place to encourage anyone to stop and wonder. Meanwhile our canals and railways, which move at a more human pace, have become the subjects of the majority of transport nostalgia, and thus leisure activity.

The major residual usage of toll-houses is as dwellings and as such they are cramped and therefore often extended; they are poorly serviced because of their remoteness and often unpleasantly sited on the highway edge. We therefore find our remaining toll-houses the unconsidered remnants of a forgotten system, infrequently listed unless tending towards the more picturesque and 'polite' and severely at risk from future road developments.

In order to celebrate what is left, we need to take the first step in recognising it. Accordingly we will now look at Somerset's turnpike roads and toll-houses in greater detail.

Boundary Stone, Chelvey Batch
Bristol Turnpike Trust
photo: janet dowding

3.0 The Somerset Turnpikes

Stagecoach and Four
(from Smith - 1970)

𝔖hepton-𝔐allet
TURNPIKE.

NOTICE IS HEREBY GIVEN,

THAT the TOLLS arising at the Toll-Gates hereinafter mentioned, will be LET by AUCTION, under Conditions to be produced, at the House of JAMES SMITH, called the BELL INN, in Shepton-Mallet, in the County of Somerset, to the best Bidder, on Monday, the Fifth Day of July next, between the Hours of Eleven in the forenoon and Two in the afternoon, in the manner directed by the Act passed in the thirteenth year of the Reign of his Majesty King George the Third, "For regulating the Turnpike Roads," which Tolls produced and were Let for, the last Year, the several Sums hereinafter mentioned and set forth, above the expence of collecting them, and they will be respectively put up at those Sums.

Whoever happens to be the best Bidder must at the same time give Security with sufficient Sureties to the satisfaction of the Trustees of the said Turnpike-Road, for Payment of the Rent agreed for, and at such times as they shall direct.

	£.	s.	D.
Butwell Gate, with the Side Gate	446	5	0
Lamyat Side Gate	32	0	0
Pecking-Mill Gate, with Side Gate and Weighbridge, and Easton-Lane Gate	247	1	0
Cannards-Grave Gate, and Foss Gate, with the Side Gate and Weighbridge	486	0	0
Downside Gate, with the Side Gate and Weighbridge, and Mendip-Road Gate	802	0	0
Stratton Gate, with the Side Gate	160	2	0
Ston-Easton Gate	360	10	0
Long-Cross Gate, with Chelynch Side Gate	200	1	0
Cranmere Gates	89	3	0
Milton Gate	81	6	0
Charlton Gate	91	5	0
Pilton Gates	71	0	0
Stean-Bow Gates	111	10	0
Glastonbury Gates	101	0	0
SUNDAY TOLLS.			
Cannards-Grave and Foss Gates	30	0	0
Downside and Mendip-Road Gates	30	0	0
Pilton Gate	6	0	0
Charlton Gate	6	0	0

By Order of the Trustees,

Dated, 7th. June, 1819.

W. Maskell, Clerk.

BURROWS and WASON, PRINTERS.

Auction of Tolls, 1819
Shepton Mallet Turnpike Trust

3.1 Somerset Turnpike Trusts

The turnpike roads came fairly early to north Somerset, with two city-centred trusts being set up in Bath and Bristol in 1707 and 1727 respectively. Whilst some of the Bath Trust's roads ventured out of Somerset into neighbouring Wiltshire, those radiating from Bristol were mainly in Gloucestershire, with a few venturing south into Somerset. The other early Somerset trust was that of 1730 covering roads into Bridgwater.

The majority of Somerset's turnpike acts, however, were passed during the boom years of the 1750's and 1760's, followed by some additional trusts in the first half of the nineteenth century. These trusts were a mixture of both linear and town-centred, the first significant venture being the 1752 trust for the road from Warminster (Wilts) to Bath, including a link to nearby Frome. This became known as the Black Dog Trust after the public house in which the trustees met. In the same year other roads from Trowbridge and Bradford (Wilts) linked into this area, whilst an act was also passed for roads into Taunton.

The following year saw activity in the south of the county with acts for roads from Sherborne to Shaftesbury (venturing into Somerset from Dorset) and from Yeovil to Axminster (Devon) via Crewkerne and Chard, roads linking Shepton Mallet and Ilchester, from Ashcott through Glastonbury and Wells towards Bristol and Bath and from Langport through Somerton towards Castle Cary. In 1756 the system was further extended in the south with another Dorset link, from Wincanton to Sherborne, along with roads into Bruton, whilst in 1757 there was more activity back in the north with acts for roads into Frome and a link from Corsham (Wilts) to Batheaston.

In the south roads around Ilminster were turnpiked in 1759, whilst in 1761 further roads from nearby South Petherton northwards to Somerton joined the system. In 1765 the roads into Crewkerne were turnpiked as were roads in the west of the county, from Minehead and Watchet. Just west of Frome the roads from Buckland Dinham to Radstock and Timsbury, largely serving the coal mining industry thereabouts, were turnpiked in 1768.

In the following less active years other trusts further extended the system by adding roads around Chard (1777), Ilchester (1778), Shepton Mallet (1780) and Wiveliscombe (1786) and from Bradford to Bathford (1792), West Harptree to Marksbury (1793) and Upottery (Devon) to Ilminster (1807). The 1820's mini-boom saw the creation of trusts for roads from High Ham over King's Sedge Moor to Ashcott (1826), and onwards from Ashcott via Wedmore to Rowberrow Hill on the Mendip ridge (1827). Finally in 1840 and 1841 respectively, links to the coast were upgraded around Weston-super-Mare and from Wells to Highbridge and Cheddar.

3.2 Deposition & Folding

The geology of Somerset is essentially a continuation north-eastwards of what is found in north Devon, where the succession of beds that continues across the rest of southern England starts, getting progressively younger as one travels east. The oldest rocks are the shales and slates laid down 400 to 350 million years ago as part of the eponymous Devonian system. These form the large mass of Exmoor that straddles north Devon and west Somerset along with the outlying Quantock Hills immediately to its east. Along the coast here the beds get progressively younger as one travels west from Somerset round into Devon. Younger rocks of Carboniferous age occur around Bampton at the start of the syncline south of Exmoor. These culm measures are variously sandstones, mudstones and shales laid down 350 to 280 million years ago when coal was being formed further north in Wales.

A similar but smaller syncline occupies the north-east corner of Somerset. Here the Devonian rocks are Old Red Sandstone and the Carboniferous a 'mountain' Limestone, which together form the heights of the Mendip ridge. In this syncline to the north these rocks dip beneath later deposits, including the coal of north Somerset, to reappear north of Bristol. This syncline continues further west beyond the Severn, where the Gower peninsula mirrors the Mendips with the south Wales coalfield immediately to its north.

The anticline that formerly sat between these two synclines is long worn away and now filled with later deposits. The oldest of these is the Permian, about 250 million years old, seen further south in Devon as bold bluffs of 'New Red Sandstone'. In Somerset these rocks form only a thin band east of Exmoor around Wiveliscombe.

Beyond this to the east Triassic rocks take over with the Keuper marls and sandstones, filling an area around Wellington and Taunton and running in bands northwards to the coast either side of the Quantocks, then westwards to Minehead and Porlock. These rocks also occur further north either side of the Mendips.

Gothick Window, Plot Stream, Aller
photo: janet dowding

3.3 Sandstone and Limestone

Further east along the coast from Watchet, the next youngest deposits in the succession can be found as the Blue Lias, Jurassic rocks laid down 180 - 140 million years ago, mainly limestones and clays that occur in a wide strip right across the country from Dorset to Yorkshire. This now coastal deposit lies at the end of a westwards pointing finger, which nearer the main strip forms the Polden Hills. Other outliers of the Lias occur slightly further north around Glastonbury, Meare, Wedmore and Brent Knoll, a series of earlier 'islands' in the sea of the later fenland of the Somerset levels. The Lias can also be found overlaying parts of the northern syncline south of Bristol burying both Triassic rocks and Carboniferous coal measures.

Later Jurassic bands which also cross the country come next in the succession to the east. The oldest and most westerly of these is the Oolitic limestone, running across Somerset from Milborne Port north to Bath and forming the Cotswold Hills further north-east. A series of limestone and clay bands overlays this further east, mostly comprising the Oxford Clay which forms a wide vale south of the Cotwolds. This runs in Somerset up the eastern boundary with Wiltshire from near Wincanton north to east of Frome.

Overlaying this in places there are in south Somerset remnants of younger rocks from the Cretaceous period 130 - 70 million years old. These comprise the Greensands of the Blackdown Hills, south of Wellington, with small patches of the younger Chalk overlying it near Chard.

In the midst of all this variety we find the Somerset levels, filling in between our two synclines where the older rocks of the anticline have been removed and their remnants now buried beneath relatively recent fenland deposits.

Although there is nothing really old, nor much recent geology, Somerset does exhibit a good range of the middle-aged rocks in the succession, providing a wide variety of building materials.

Gothick Window, Butwell
photo: janet dowding

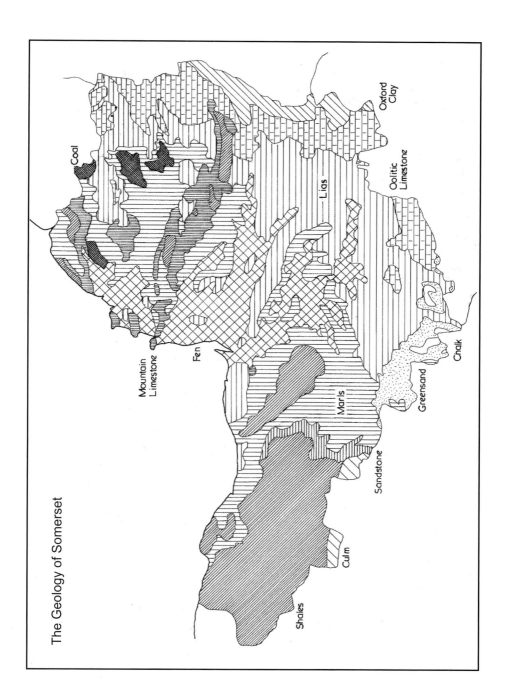

The Geology of Somerset

3.4 Somerset Toll-houses

That Somerset's toll-houses are many is witnessed by the sheer size of the gazetteer filling the latter part of this book; that they are varied by the fact that no two seem the same. They range in size from the unusually large example at Shuttern (Taunton), which also accommodated the Trust's offices, to the single room toll-booth at Clewer on the Somerset levels, which probably had separate living accommodation adjoining.

They range in plan shape from the rectangular to the polygonal, with interesting variants in between the two. Two storey rectangular toll-houses are common, those with a small side window revealing their purpose less so, examples being found in Beam Bridge (Taunton) and Chilkwell Street (Glastonbury). Sometimes the small window can be found in the porch as at Shutteroaks (Crewkerne) and Bull's Bridge (Frome).

Visibility was certainly important, both in respect of the toll-gate keeper having a view up and down the road as well as for approaching travellers getting the impression they had been spotted from the windows. This was achieved on some rectangular toll-houses by the addition of a small bay window, such as seen at Penstile (Yeovil) and Soho (Frome).

A development of this is the single storey rectangular toll-house with a projecting canted bay which included the door as well as side windows. This design was much used by Telford in Scotland and can also be found in the fens of west Norfolk. Good examples in Somerset were built by the Bath Trust (Red Post and Corston) and by the Langport Trust (Kingsbury and Muchelney). The first three have square headed windows with drip mouldings over, the last 'gothick' pointed ones.

The use of such a canted bay, partly octagonal in plan, signalling the toll-house building's purpose became more prevalent in Victorian times and was used on the canals as well as the roads.

'Telford' type toll-house
Muchelney, Langport
photo: janet dowding

On some two storey buildings this bay appeared asymmetrically as a full height projection towards the road somewhere on the longer side of a rectangular plan, as at Wembdon (Bridgwater) or East Cranmore (Shepton Mallet). However, such a bay added to the shorter side of a rectangular plan leads to an octagonal ended toll-house, where the bay itself is all there is to the end elevation facing the road. Somerset has its fair share of these with good examples at Nether Stowey (Minehead), South Cheriton (Blackmoor), Plot Stream (Langport) and Swainswick (Bath).

There is a fully octagonal toll-house at Exebridge, south of Minehead and the perhaps unique hexagonal example at Stanton Drew, pictured on many a postcard. The 'picturesque' style was enhanced by the use of 'gothick' pointed windows, good examples of which can be found at Snowdon Hill (Chard), Easthams (Crewkerne) and Butwell (Castle Cary), all set within walls of local stone adding to the effect.

The other nineteenth century tradition, the Classical, is less prevalent in toll-houses, but does appear to good effect in the more urban centres of Bath and Bristol. A fine example survives at Ashton (Bristol), where the usual part octagonal plan shape has become semi-circular.

Another overlay of variety is provided by Somerset's rich resources of local stone, mostly good for building. The majority of the toll-houses so far mentioned have been of local stone, sometimes rendered, and with slate roofs, as might be expected with such good roofing material not too far away.

Indeed the toll-house at Chard Borough is unusually slate-hung, as if transplanted from further west, whilst not too far away that at Snowdon Hill has walls of pebbles (from the chalk) with brick dressings and a thatched roof.

Classical style toll-house
Saltford, Bristol
photo: janet dowding

27

4.0 A Somerset Gazetteer

The remainder of this book comprises a gazetteer of both toll-houses and their former sites. In general all surviving toll-houses are illustrated and have a map reference without brackets. Those that have been lost are also illustrated where a suitable photograph has been forthcoming, but are given bracketed map references. The remaining toll-house sites, lost without trace other than documentary, are described as far as possible in the text boxes.

'T.P.' and 'T.G.' indicate turnpike or toll-gate as shown on the first edition 1" OS maps originating c.1809 but updated through the 19th Century (many of them showing railway routes as well), whilst 'T.B.' is toll-bar as shown on Greenwood's 1822 Somerset maps. The gazetteer starts in the far west of Somerset around Minehead and runs roughly north-eastwards through the main town-centred and linear trusts, ending in the north around Bath and Bristol at the borders with Wiltshire and Gloucestershire respectively.

The authors are very conscious of this being a first attempt to document these buildings in such detail and would be very grateful to hear of any errors, omissions, additional information or photographic evidence in respect of any toll-house that readers might be aware of. If enough new information is uncovered, a second updated edition may well be justified in due course.

Readers should be aware that most of our surviving toll-houses are now in private ownership as people's homes; please respect this. The authors apologise in advance to any owners for any nuisance this publication might bring their way, and hope the benefits of wider knowledge of this obscure subject can be seen to outweigh any inconvenience caused.

It is certainly hoped that a good many owners will come to appreciate their guardianship of this small part of our heritage, and perhaps a few more of these unique buildings will in due course get the added protection of becoming listed buildings.

Milestone, Blagdon Hill
photo: janet dowding

28

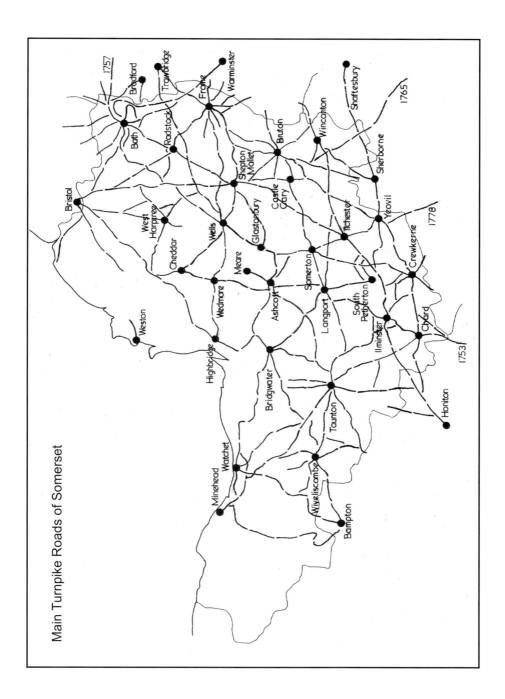

Main Turnpike Roads of Somerset

Date	Act	Turnpike
1707	6 A c.42	Roads into Bath
1727	13 GI c.12	Roads into Bristol
1730	3 GII c.34	Roads into Bridgwater
1743	16 GII c.22	Cirencester - Bath
1752	25 GII c.12	Warminster - Bath etc. (Black Dog)
1752	25 GII c.17	Seend - Trowbridge - Beckington
1752	25 GII c.24	Trowbridge - Edington etc.
1752	25 GII c.52	Combe Bridge - Bradford
1752	25 GII c.54	Roads into Taunton
1753	26 GII c.60	Sherborne - Shaftesbury
1753	26 GII c.69	Roads around Yeovil
1753	26 GII c.71	Shepton Mallet & Ilchester
1753	26 GII c.76	Ashcott - Glastonbury - Wells etc.
1753	26 GII c.92	Langport - Somerton - Castle Cary
1756	29 GII c.49	Roads around Wincanton
1756	29 GII c.50	Roads into Bruton
1757	30 GII c.39	Roads into Frome
1757	30 GII c.46	Corsham - Batheaston Bridge
1759	32 GII c.39	Roads around Ilminster
1761	1 GIII c.29	South Petherton - Martock - Somerton
1765	5 GIII c.61	Roads into Crewkerne
1765	5 GIII c.75	Roads into Honiton
1765	5 GIII c.93	Roads from Minehead etc.
1765	5 GIII c.102	Blandford - Bratton (Vale of Blackmoor)
1768	8 GIII c.53	Buckland Dinham - Radstock etc.
1777	17 GIII c.89	Roads around Chard
1778	18 GIII c.95	Barwick - Charminster etc. (Maiden Newton)
1778	18 GIII c.101	Roads into Ilchester
1780	20 GIII c.85	Roads into Shepton Mallet
1786	26 GIII c.135	Roads into Wiveliscombe
1792	32 GIII c.137	Bradford - Bathford Bridge
1793	33 GIII c.165	West Harptree - Marksbury etc.
1807	47 GIII c.6	Upottery - Ilminster
1826	7 GIV c.39	Langport - Meare (High Ham & Ashcott)
1827	7/8 GIV c.5	Ashcott - Wedmore - Rowberrow
1840	3/4 V c.22	Roads around Weston-super-Mare
1841	4/5 V c.98	Wells - Highbridge & Cheddar

Main Turnpike Acts of Somerset

Exebridge Toll-house
SS 932242
Roads from Minehead etc.

photo: janet dowding

This octagonal toll-house still stands on the Somerset/Devon border, replacing an earlier one on the old Minehead to Bampton turnpike road (now B3222). This probably stood adjoining the actual bridge and the new position was required by a junction with the later 1828 road.

The new toll-house is grade II listed and retains its small porch and a recess at first floor which could have held the toll-board.

Under the Minehead Turnpike Bill the annual income for this gate was estimated at £250 and the toll-keeper's wages would have been 5 shillings per week. In 1871 this position was held by Elizabeth Elliott, living there with her three daughters.

Weare Toll-hut
(SS 937267)
Roads from Minehead etc.

The erection of more gates was a trust's only method of increasing income and by 1839 an additional gate had been erected at Weare, north of Exebridge, where a side road led to Weir Bridge and on to a nearby sawmill.

This was on the new 1828 road (now A396) and was not served by a toll-house, rather a toll-hut, providing basic shelter for the gate-keeper. It was still there in 1866, but in the 1877 sale would have been cleared from the land, which reverted to its original owner.

Chilly Bridge Toll-house, Brompton Regis
SS 924307
Roads from Minehead etc.

photo: janet dowding

The road south from Timberscombe to the Devon border (now A396) had been authorised by a turnpike act in 1822. Accordingly Chilly Bridge gate was erected after 1824, two miles south of Bridgetown, at the junction of a lane to Dulverton.

This plain rectangular toll-house served the gate and remains today with a small side window for the better observation of traffic from the north. In 1871 the 'gate keeper' was 50 year old Ann Farmer, living there with her husband and two children.

This was one of ten toll-houses owned by the Minehead Trust at its demise in 1877, but does not appear in the auction notice of 1 September that year and may have been sold separately.

Dulverton Toll-house
(SS 915279)
Roads from Minehead etc.

Dulverton 'Turnpike Gate House' stood on the original 1765 Minehead to Bampton turnpike road, replaced in 1827 by the new road (now A396) but not then disturnpiked.

In the 1770's a gate had been erected on Vicarage Hill at the top of the town, apparently near the present Congregational Church.

In 1871 the Census records 'gate keeper and schoolmistress' 57 year old Ann Cole, living there with her 'dressmaker' daughter Emily. The house was sold for £28 in 1877, when the trust was wound up.

Dunster Toll-house
SS 988434
Roads from Minehead etc.

photo: janet dowding

On the original Minehead to Bampton road, turnpiked in 1765 (now the A396), the northernmost of the four gates was erected at Dunster. At the west end of the village the toll-house survives, albeit enlarged, at 38 West Street, the last in the village and known as 'Toll Cottage'.

It was shown in the 1871 Census as between West Street and Frackford, with 51 year old 'toll gate keeper' Maria Vickery, her daughter and grandson living there.

It was included in the 1866 tally of gates of the Minehead Trust, but appears to have been disposed of separately from the toll-gates and posts that were auctioned in 1877.

Green Dragon Stop-gate, Bilbrook
(ST 037410)
Roads from Minehead etc.

Set up in 1825 to control a side turning, the Green Dragon Stop-gate did not collect tolls from the main Minehead to Nether Stowey turnpike road dating from 1765.

By 1866 1s. 6d. per week was being paid to the stop-gate keeper, but it is unclear whether there was a toll-house here or not. Although recorded as Green Dragon 'Stop-gate' in the late 1860's, the materials of a Green Dragon 'Toll-house' were sold off at the 1 September 1877 auction at Washford.

Four Lost Minehead Toll-houses

Roads from Minehead etc.

Wheddon Cross Toll-house
(SS 924388)
Roads from Minehead etc.

Wheddon Cross is situated on the watershed between the north flowing River Avill and the southbound River Quarme. The new road built in 1822-28 southwards from Minehead to Exebridge followed these valleys and is now the A396.

The toll-house was built after 1824 and occupied in 1871 by 72 year old 'toll gate keeper' Elizabeth Stevens.

On 1 September 1877 the materials for the toll-house were auctioned off at Washford and the land was cleared and reverted to its previous owner. The toll-gates and posts were sold separately.

Louisa Gate, Bury Hill
(SS 937287)
Roads from Minehead etc.

A somewhat short-lived turnpike gate on the original 1765 road, Louisa Gate was abolished in 1824 when the old route southwards over the hills between Timberscombe and Hele Bridge was disturnpiked.

The site is still marked on modern OS maps, but appeared on the first edition OS as 'Lousy Gate'.

Alcombe Cross Toll-house
(SS 976452)   'T.G.'
Roads from Minehead etc.

This first toll-house out of Minehead on the road to Nether Stowey was built in 1824. Near the London Inn in what was once a village separate from Minehead, there were both main and side gates here.

In 1871 the 'toll collector' was Mary Gardener and in 1877 the house was auctioned and along with its outbuildings it made £136. However no trace remains today of this toll-house.

Timberscombe Toll-house
(SS 956426)   'T Pike'
Roads from Minehead etc.

The original 1765 route from Minehead southwards to the Devon border went through Dunster and then Timberscombe before taking to the hills east of the river valleys via Heath Poult Cross on Quarme Hill. This site at Cowbridge was an obvious one for a second gate along this route, as it controlled access from across the river, where a stop-gate at Knowle had caught teams of packhorses avoiding payment.

In 1871 the Census recorded 36 year old 'toll collector' Mary Lyddon at the house, with her 'tailor' husband Thomas and four children.

Carhampton Toll-house
ST 002432   'T Pike'
Roads from Minehead etc.

photo: janet dowding

After Alcombe Gate, the next gate along the 1765 Minehead to Nether Stowey turnpike road was near Carhampton. Sited at the south-eastern end of a modern road diversion on the A39 near Paradise Farm, it was at one time known as Paradise Toll-house.

The existing cottage on the site shown above is believed to be the original toll-house, and the various side windows in the gable end support this assumption.

A 4½d. ticket purchased at Carhampton also gave passage through Alcombe Gate, the last before Minehead itself. In 1861 the 'toll collector' was Frederick Kilmer, living there with his ten year old son Charles.

Washford Toll-house
(ST 047411)
Roads from Minehead etc.

Washford was on the original 1765 Minehead to Nether Stowey road, but the improved route through the village probably dates from the 1828 Act. In addition the Washford to Bishops Lydeard road was turnpiked in 1807.

In 1825 a new gate had been set up in Washford, joined by a second one in 1839 and by 1866 there existed Washford West, South and Stop gates, the keeper at the latter being paid 1s. 6d. a week. In 1871 the 'toll collector' was 59 year old James Newman.

Blue Anchor Toll-house, Old Cleeve
ST 033435   'T.B.'
Roads from Minehead etc.

photo: janet dowding

Situated on the coast road between Carhampton and Watchet (now B3191), adjacent to the turning inland to Old Cleeve, this toll-house controlled part of the original 1765 turnpike road.

It survives, but much altered in recent times, probably a result of its plain double-fronted design, not leading to a listing. Old photographs show it without dormers and with a central porch and a chimney at both gables.

Its income was always low, weekly receipts varying from a shilling to 2½d. over the years, leading in 1825 to its abandonment and sale. It seems very little traffic originated in Watchet for Minehead.

West Gate, Watchet
(ST 067435)
Roads from Minehead etc.

The road west from Watchet was controlled by a gate in West Street, probably close outside the built up area, possibly near Jubilee Terrace on the Blue Anchor road.

Another poor performer, receipts from Watchet West Gate in 1771 were insufficient to cover expenses and in 1777 it made only £10. In 1825 its income was much the same but it was retained, however by 1866 only two shillings a week was being taken by the gatekeeper.

Five Bells Toll-house, Watchet
(ST 065423)   'T.G.'
Roads from Minehead etc.

photo: watchet market house museum

As a result of the 1786 Turnpike Bill, several toll-gates were erected within the boundaries of Watchet, guarding routes to the west, south and east. In 1828 this new angle fronted toll-house at Five Bells, replaced the southern gate. It stood at the crossing of two roads and was a well known landmark until its demolition in the 1950's to improve visibility for motorists.

In 1871 the 'toll gate keeper' was Ann Young aged 32. The two gates at Five Bells were apparently the most valuable in the Dunster District, the reserve price for them at an auction of tolls in 1872 being £302. At the abolition of the Minehead Trust in 1877, the Five Bells toll-house was one of ten auctioned off.

South-east Gate, Watchet
(ST 073432)   'T.B.'
Roads from Minehead etc.

One of three original Watchet gates, this one at Windwhistle Cross, more commonly known as the Pound, was on the original 1765 turnpike road from Minehead to Nether Stowey.

The site is at the corner of the present South Road and St Decuman's Road and was shown as 'T.B.' on Greenwood's 1822 map of Somerset's roads.

It was replaced by Doniford Gate after 1828.

More Lost Minehead Toll-houses

Roads from Minehead etc.

Fair Cross Toll-house
(ST 054396)
Roads from Minehead etc.

Fair Cross is where the old 1765 Taunton road from Washford via Monksilver is crossed by the present day B3190 road southwards from Watchet towards Bampton in Devon.

However the toll-house there was not built until 1862, after the opening of the Taunton to Watchet railway, in the hope that traffic there would be less affected by the new system.

In 1871 31 year old John Penny and his wife Thirza were toll keepers in 'Tollgate House'.

Yard Mills Stop Gate
(ST 060392)
Roads from Minehead etc.

About half a mile south-east of Fair Cross towards Taunton, there was a further gate set up following the opening of the Taunton to Watchet railway in 1862. It supported the Fair Cross gate, but had no toll-house, just a hut for the collector.

The takings at this gate were always meagre, the new Williton to Taunton road having starved it of traffic. The toll-box from Yard Mills was auctioned off in 1877 separate from the gates and posts.

Robbery Gate Toll-house,
(ST 014333)   **Brendon Hills**
Roads from Minehead etc.

Known variously as Robbery or Rodborough Gate, this site was near present day Roborough Gate Farm on the B3190. This road from Watchet to Lowtrow Cross was turnpiked in 1765 and continued southwards to Bampton in Devon.

In about 1825 the house at Rodborough Gate was sold off and a new gate called Brendon Hill was erected a mile further south. A number of old tracks in this area suggest there was some evasion of tolls happening.

Brendon Hill Toll-house
(ST 008321)   'T.Pike'
Roads from Minehead etc.

Built to replace Robbery Gate, this toll-house appeared as 'T.Pike' on the first edition 1" OS maps. In 1841 it was occupied by 'ag.lab' John Osgood, aged 40, along with his wife and four children.

The gate was let jointly with that at Ragland Castle and in 1866 it also had a side-gate, presumably covering a track down into Middleton Bottom. Although one of the ten houses owned by this trust it did not appear at auction in 1877, probably having been sold separately.

Ashbeer Toll-house, Stogumber
ST 087359
Roads from Minehead etc.

photo: janet dowding

Ashbeer Toll-house still stands at an isolated spot on Silverdown Hill about a mile and a half south-east of Monksilver. It was on the old 1765 turnpike road from Washford south over the hills towards Wiveliscombe, superseded by the later route of c.1806 up the river valley (present day B3188).

The toll-house was near the end of this trust's responsibilities and is very similar to the one at Blue Anchor, remaining a little less altered, a plain double-fronted cottage with a large porch. Since this photograph was taken the toll-house has unfortunately suffered a fire and is currently boarded up with scaffolding.

Monksilver Toll-gate,
(ST 075374)   'T.B.'
Roads from Minehead etc.

On Greenwood's 1822 map a 'T.B.' is shown at Monksilver on the old 1765 turnpike road from Washford to Hartrow Gate.

When the proceeds of this gate for the coming year were auctioned in 1827/8 they fetched £181, but by 1829 this was only £11, receipts having fallen dramatically.

It survived for a few more years, but clearly the old Taunton road was no longer popular as the site does not appear in the 1841 Census.

Long Street Toll-house, Williton
ST 079413
Roads from Minehead etc.

photo: janet dowding

Now known as 'Old Toll House', the building at the eastern end of this terrace was reputedly used during the 19th Century as a toll-house. The west end served as an office for the Wyndham Estate, the original thatch having been replaced with pantiles in the 1930's.

In Long Street, Williton, it certainly stands on the line of the old 1765 Minehead to Nether Stowey road, but is not mentioned in the 1866 tally of gates, nor the 1877 auction.

An interesting mention of this gate appears in some local histories: apparently a circus elephant lifted the gate off its hinges and walked through whilst its owner was arguing about the charge due.

> **Doniford Toll-house**
> (ST 088428)
> *Roads from Minehead etc.*
>
> After 1828, Doniford Gate replaced the South-east Gate at Windwhistle, Watchet on the original 1765 route from Minehead to Nether Stowey. By 1829 there was also a new stop gate at the north end of Watery Lane, Doniford, which was still there in the tally of 1866.
>
> In 1851 the 'toll gate keeper' was 62 year old Elizabeth Perry, and by 1866 she would have earned just 2 shillings a week.
>
> The Doniford toll-house was one of the ten sold off at auction in 1877.

Tower Hill Toll-house, Williton
ST 079408
Roads from Minehead etc.

photo: janet dowding

The Washford to Bishop's Lydeard road was turnpiked under the 1807 Act and around 1825/26 a new gate was established at Williton called Tower Hill. This rendered building with a slate roof at the junction of Bridge Street, High Street and Tower Hill is known as 'Toll Cottage' and is most probably the toll-house concerned.

It was profitable, with tolls soon amounting to about £150 per year, although this was probably at the expense of those at Ragland Castle gate, about half a mile further along this road.

In 1861 this 'toll gate' was occupied by Mary Rogers, aged 36, a widow with two sons at home.

Ragland Castle Toll-house
(ST 085405)
Roads from Minehead etc.

Like Tower Hill, the gate at Ragland Castle, a little further south-east of Williton at Sampford Brett, was included in the 1866 tally of Minehead Trust gates.

It did not however figure in the 1877 auction at the Trust's demise, as it was reputedly ceremonially burned by a party led by fish porter Olly, well known locally for his opposition to the trust. Receipts here were probably poor due to the nearness of the Tower Hill gate.

Even More Lost Minehead Toll-houses

Roads from Minehead etc.

Wibble Lane Toll-house, Williton
(ST 092418)
Roads from Minehead etc.

The Wibble Lane toll-house stood at a place called Black George, on the 1807 turnpike road north-eastwards from Williton towards Rydon cross-roads, where that road joined the original 1765 coastal road from Watchet.

To the immediate east of Black George, a new road was authorised under the later 1828 Act involving alterations around St Audrie's, this becoming the present day A39. The old road from Wibble Lane Gate to Rydon Cross became disused, remaining as a well preserved example of turnpike road until recently concreted to give access to a landfill site.

In 1861 'Wibble Turnpike Gate' was occupied by 'gatekeeper' Elizabeth Elliot with her 'ag.lab' husband and four children.

Seven Ash Toll-gate
(ST 152333)
Roads from Minehead etc.

Between 1824 and 1826, money was raised for a second Taunton road a few miles north-east of the 1807 route from Washford to Bishop's Lydeard via Monksilver. The route ran parallel to Doniford Stream in the river valley below the ridge of the Quantock Hills and is now the A358.

The gates established at Seven Ash and East Coombe however yielded a poor return, only £28 on first letting and still only £52 in 1833, despite the addition of gates at Dull Cross.

Shortly after the opening of the Taunton to Watchet railway in 1862, again parallel to the river and mostly within one mile of this road, the Minehead trustees took down the Seven Ash and Dull Cross gates and concentrated their efforts on the old road at Fair Cross and Yard Mills.

Shutgate Toll-house, Williton
(ST 077413)
Roads from Minehead etc.

Sometime before the 1860's a toll-house stood in Shutgate (now North) Street, Williton. In 1866 the Mason's Arms was built on the site, but nothing more is known.

East Coombe Toll-gate
(ST 161311)
Roads from Minehead etc.

The East Coombe gate was included in the 1866 tally of gates along with a side gate. In 1861, 69 year old widower George Perry was 'turnpike toll collector' there.

Putsham Toll-house, Kilve
(ST 148429)
Roads from Minehead etc.

photo: somerset county council

This old photograph shows the Putsham toll-house in the village of Kilve, towards the eastern end of the Minehead to Nether Stowey turnpike road of 1765. Demolished to make way for the entrance to the village car park, it was fortunately recorded for posterity.

There is however some dispute locally about its exact position, some preferring sites further east along this road. In 1851 the 'toll collector' was 74 year old Alexander Perry. It was included in the 1866 tally of gates for the Minehead Trust, but only the gates were auctioned off in 1877, the house presumably disposed of separately.

Elworthy Cross Toll-house
(ST 086347)
Roads into Wiveliscombe

The toll-house at Elworthy Cross, two miles south of Monksilver on the present day B3188, was just south of the village of Elworthy. Here a minor road crosses the Watchet to Wiveliscombe road, both of which were turnpiked in 1806.

There were gates on each road except that leading to the village. A parallel route between Brompton Ralph and Stogumber which ran east of Elworthy avoiding the toll-house, was called Save Penny Lane but only lasted until 1827.

In 1841 the toll-house was occupied by carpenter James Slade, aged 45.

Nether Stowey Toll-house
ST 193397
Roads from Minehead etc.

photo: janet dowding

This late 18th Century grade II listed toll-house still stands at 15 St Mary's Street, Nether Stowey. It is built of local stone with brick dressings and has a classic angled front with 'gothick' pointed door and window heads, hipped tiled roof and tall chimney stack.

On the original 1765 turnpike road from Minehead, its position within the village has probably saved it, as the by-pass now takes the A39 around to the north. At the eastern end of the village the Minehead Trust ended and the Bridgwater Trust took over as recorded on an old stone in the wall of Vicarage House which reads "Here ends Bridgewater road" (sic).

In addition to Stowey Gate, there were two others known as Jackson's Lane Gate and Limekiln Lane Gate added c.1825, all three being let together according to a parliamentary report of 1840. The 1866 tally of gates for this trust also indicates a side-gate here. In 1871 the 'toll gate keeper' was 47 year old Maria Woolcott, unmarried and living there alone.

In 1877 all three sets of gates and posts were auctioned off, as were the materials of the Nether Stowey toll-house. Presumably the latter were bought by the landowner to which the site had reverted, so that demolition did not occur.

Wembdon West Toll-house
ST 276379
Roads into Bridgwater

photo: janet dowding

Known as 'Toll Gate House' this substantial pink-painted building is situated just off the B3339 at the western end of Wembdon in what is now Skimmerton Lane, but possibly Salmon Lane in the 19th Century.

Of two storeys with a projecting canted bay with side windows, the original porch and doorway, shown on a 19th Century drawing, have now gone. The space over the door for a toll-board remains.

In 1861 the 'toll collector' was Thomas Evans, aged 24, living there with his wife Elizabeth and their son and nephew. It has obviously been enlarged, but probably survives because of its position in what is now a quiet secluded rural lane.

Sandford Waters Toll-house,
(ST 270382)   **Cannington**
Roads into Bridgwater

According to Somerset Historic Environment Record, there was reputedly a toll-house at the Sandford Waters junction, west of Wembdon and Bridgwater, on the road originally turnpiked in 1730 from Bawdrip to Cannington.

A 'gate keeper' is recorded in 1841 and a 'toll bar keeper' in 1851, Thomas Batt aged 62, living there with his wife Sarah. There is however no entry for the toll-house in 1861 so it may have ceased to function by then, possibly replaced by Wembdon West.

Wembdon East Toll-house
ST 288373   'T.Pike' 'T.B.'
Roads into Bridgwater

photo: janet dowding

This second surviving toll-house in the village of Wembdon, west of Bridgwater, is known as 'Old Toll House'. It is in the middle of the village on the 1730 turnpike road from Cannington to Bawdrip (B3339) and was shown by Greenwood in 1822 as 'T.B.' and on the first edition 1" OS map as 'T.Pike'.

Now a plain two storey cottage, it was shown in an old photograph from c.1850 with a small porch on the front facing the road and the gates, the doorway now replaced by a window.

In 1861 the 'tollgate keeper' was 42 year old Priscilla Pugsley, a widow with three daughters and a son living there.

Dunball Gate Toll-house, Puriton
(approx ST 315415)
Roads into Bridgwater

The original road from Bridgwater to Bristol ran via Crandon Bridge and was turnpiked in 1730 as far as Puriton. The remaining length to East Brent, joining up with the Bristol Trust, followed in 1759.

It is impossible to tell from the old names on the Census entries exactly where the toll-house stood near the village of Puriton, but if not at the turn for Dunball, it could have been at the top of Puriton Hill (ST 322410). The 'toll collector' in 1861 was James Burnett, aged 46 and living there alone.

Durleigh Hill Toll-house, Bridgwater
(approx ST 291365)   'T.B.'
Roads into Bridgwater

photo: blake museum, bridgwater

The road from Bridgwater to Enmore was turnpiked in 1730 and extended further south-westwards to Bishops Lydeard in 1759. Greenwood in 1822 shows a 'T.B.' on Durleigh Hill (now Durleigh Road) just outside the Bridgwater town limits.

Now long gone, fortunately the toll-house was recorded in this 19th Century photograph showing a horse rider at the toll-gates. The toll-house was a simple two storey cottage with a corner chimney and its gable facing the road. In addition to the porch there is a toll-board on the wall and a lamp bracket at first floor level.

East Toll-house, Wiveliscombe
(ST 085277)
Roads into Wiveliscombe

East Turnpike Gate adjoined the junction of Frog Street (now Ford Road) and Milverton Road (now Taunton Road). Maps attached to estate sales notices for lots in the town for 1834 and 1838 clearly show 'Turnpike Gate' and a substantial toll-house with a small bay facing south and a gate across the road, also shown on old maps of 1816 and 1841.

In 1851 'East Turnpike Gate' was occupied by 'Turnpike Gate Keeper' William Trenchard, a widower aged 63. Not shown on the 1887 OS map, the toll-house is believed to have been demolished after the demise of the Trust in 1871.

Monmouth Street Toll-house, Bridgwater
ST 304374
Roads into Bridgwater

photo: janet dowding

This grade II listed toll-house survives at the junction of the Bath and Bristol roads (now A38 and A39) north-eastwards out of Bridgwater. Built between 1820 and 1840, at 43 Monmouth Street, it is of two storeys with a symmetrical three window range, the two ground floor windows having Tudor-arched heads.

A 19th Century photograph shows it originally had drip mouldings over all the windows and a substantial central porch with side windows for better observation of traffic and a very large lamp beside the porch door.

In 1851 the toll collector was L. Bonning aged 33, living there with his wife and 2 year old daughter Georgina.

Hartswell Toll-house,
(ST 081273)　　　　　**Wiveliscombe**
Roads into Wiveliscombe

Marked on an 1816 Prebendal Manor map, there was a toll-house at Hartswell, on the road south of Wiveliscombe to Langford Budville and Whiteball turnpiked in 1786.

It stood at the junction of this road and the old road (now nothing more than a track on modern maps) out of Wiveliscombe to Fleed which was used before the newer road of the 1820's was built (now B3227).

In 1851 the 'Turnpike Gate Keeper' there was Samuel Allen, aged 25, and unmarried.

Taunton Road Toll-house, Bridgwater
ST 301363   'T Pike'   'T.B.'
Roads into Bridgwater

photo: janet dowding

Another substantial grade II listed Bridgwater toll-house stands on the line of the original Taunton road turnpiked in 1730 (now A38). It is early 19th Century in date of painted brick and not believed to have been substantially altered.

Known as 'Old Toll House', 103 Taunton Road has an oriel window over the front door in the stepped forward central block with narrow windows to the returns of the bay. The garden wall is built of redundant Bath bricks.

In 1861 the 'toll collector' was 47 year old bachelor Thomas Lovering.

Langley Toll-house, Wiveliscombe
(ST 079283)   'T.B.'
Roads into Wiveliscombe

Greenwood's 1822 map and an 1816 Prebendal Manor map of Wiveliscombe both show a toll-gate close to the junction of Greenway Lane in the area now known as Northgate. This road was turnpiked in 1786 and ran from Four Cross Ways (on B3190) via Huish Champflower into Wiveliscombe.

In 1851 'Lessee of turnpike tolls' there was James Manning, aged 31, but in 1861 'Langley Gate, Greenway' was occupied by William Collard, a mason, with his wife and family. In 1871 they were all still there with Sarah Ann, his wife, acting as 'Toll Gate Keeper'.

Three Lost Wiveliscombe Toll-houses

Roads into Wiveliscombe

Waterrow Toll-house
(ST 052254)
Roads into Wiveliscombe

Somerset's Historic Environment Record includes a turnpike house at Waterrow shown on a plan of Hurstone in 1848 (a side road from Waterrow leads to Hurstone Farm).

Waterrow is on the 'New Road' from Wiveliscombe towards South Molton, authorised by the 1806 Act but not started or completed until the 1820's. The toll-house must therefore have dated from about 1824, but it has now gone. The site is across the bridge from the Rock Inn, actually in one of the inn's car parks.

Tolland Toll-house
(ST 097322)
Roads into Wiveliscombe

The present day B3188 northwards from Wiveliscombe was turnpiked in 1786 as far as Elworthy.

Two miles short of the end there is evidence for a toll-house at Tolland in the 1841 and 1871 Census entries. These show respectively 'Turnpike House' and 'Tolland Toll House', shown as situated between 'Parks' and 'Smith Cottage/Smith Close'.

West Toll-house, Wiveliscombe
(approx ST 076277)   'T.B.' 'T.G.'
Roads into Wiveliscombe

The West Turnpike Gate in Wiveliscombe stood on the present day B3227 just to the west of the town. The toll-gate was at the foot of Farmers Cleave where the first edition 1" OS map shows a 'T.G.' and Greenwood (1822) shows a 'T.B.'. Since the new road authorised in 1806 was not actually built until the 1820's, it remains unclear if the site is an older one as shown on a Deposited Plan of 1823/24 or whether it was built as a result of the 'New Road'. It is thought that the turnpike road out of the town went via West Street and West Road, Croft Way being a modern relief road.

The 1851 Census, when William Priscott aged 36, tailor and gatekeeper, was living in the toll-house, shows it to be close to Farmer's Cleeve on one side and 'Almshouses' on the other. The 1871 census also shows 'Turnpike Gate West' as near 'Almshouses'.

Ford Toll-house
ST 091285
Roads into Wiveliscombe

photo: janet dowding

This building is believed to be the surviving toll-house at Ford, a hamlet one mile north-east of Wiveliscombe on the original 1786 road towards Watchet. On Ridge Hill, at its junction with Grant's Lane leading to Langley, it was known as both 'Lower Ridge Turnpike Gate House' and 'Grant's Gate Toll House', but is now simply Ford Gate Cottage.

The toll-house, now a plain looking cottage facing on to the road, may once have had a porch between the two lower windows. In 1871 'Ford Turnpike Gate' was occupied by 35 year old Sarah Stevens, her labourer husband and their three children. At the end of the turnpike era, the house was conveyed by the trust on 2 May 1871 to the Hancock family for £25.

Pitsford Hill Toll-house,
(ST 099306)   **Brompton Ralph**
Roads into Wiveliscombe

Further north on the road towards Watchet was Pitsford Hill Gate, shown on an 1809 map as being immediately north of the Fitzhead road junction at ST 099306. It may have been moved farther south nearer Ford gate, when the small section of road from Pitsford Hill to Burrow Hill Farm was improved, but there would have been no need for two toll-houses so close together.

In 1871 the Pitsford Hill toll-house was occupied by Henry Briddle, aged 27, his wife and two small sons.

Lost Toll-houses near Milverton

Roads into Wiveliscombe

Milverton Toll-house
(ST 124259)
Roads into Wiveliscombe

The roads around Milverton were managed by two separate trusts thought to have met at Rock Corner, the junction of North Street and Silver Street, where a toll-house stood. The Taunton Trust of 1752 controlled the road to the east, whilst the later Wiveliscombe Trust of 1786 controlled the road to the west and that south from Milverton through Langford Gate, and further on to Wellington in 1806.

The toll-house is shown on the 1842 tithe map and the 1871 Census shows Mary Perrott, aged 63, as 'toll gate keeper'.

Langford Budville Toll-house
(ST 115232)
Roads into Wiveliscombe

Langford Gate (also shown as Chipley Gate on early OS maps) was on the original Milverton to White Ball road turnpiked in 1786. The present day B3187 from Milverton still passes through, but follows the 1806 route onwards to Tone Bridge, Wellington.

The toll-house stood at the junction of these two roads east of Langford Budville village. In 1871 the 'turnpike gate' was occupied by 51 year old widow Mary Matthews, 'toll collector', and her three unmarried daughters.

Roads into Tiverton

Runnington Toll-house
(approx ST 122223)
Roads into Wiveliscombe

The Runnington Turnpike Gate probably stood adjoining the junction of the present day B3187 and the road to Runnington village, 'Sandylands' on modern maps.

This stretch of road from Langford Gate to Tone Bridge, Wellington, was turnpiked in 1806. The 1871 Census places it next to 'Sandylane House' with Eliza Stevens, a widow aged 49, as 'Turnpike Gate Keeper', living there with her son Samuel, a 17 year old 'ag.lab'.

White Ball Gate Toll-house
(ST 090185)   'T.B.'
Roads into Tiverton

The Taunton and Tiverton trusts met at the Whiteball Inn (ST 099188) and a short distance south-west down the turnpike road stood White Ball Gate. Greenwood's 1822 map shows two 'T.B.'s there, one on the county boundary, where Longwood Lane and Gipsy Lane join the main road (now A38), the other further into Somerset at ST 093186, where the road from Gamlins Farm joins.

The toll-house must have controlled both gates. The name 'White Ball Gate' still survives on modern OS maps although the toll-house has long gone.

Beam Bridge Toll-house, Sampford Arundel
ST 108194   'T.B.'   'T.G.'
Roads into Taunton

photo: janet dowding

Although the roads around Beam Bridge have been altered extensively during the 20th Century, a small section of the original 1752 turnpike road remains here parallel to the main road, together with Beam Bridge toll-house. This latter, which was also known as Sampford Gate, is a substantial dwelling, now somewhat altered and enlarged.

Greenwood's 1822 map shows a 'T.B.' here and the 1871 Census records Sarah Gambyn, aged 55, as 'toll keeper' and places the toll-house near the Beam Bridge Inn. A milestone against the southern wall saying 'Taunton 9 miles' is believed to have been moved here from its original site.

> **Wellington South Toll-house**
> (ST 136204)   'T.B.'
> *Roads into Taunton*
>
> The main road through Wellington, one of the most important in the county, was turnpiked in 1752 by the Taunton Trust and in 1809 two toll-gates were erected in the town.
>
> Greenwood, 1822, shows a 'T.B.' at the junction of the main road (now Mantle Street) with the side road (now Champford Lane). Apparently the toll-keeper's cottage was almost in the middle of the road.
>
> In 1851 'Turnpike Gate House' was occupied by Charlotte Adams, 'gate keeper', and her seven children.

Lost Toll-houses near Wellington

Roads into Taunton

Wellington North Toll-house
(ST 142209)   'T.B.'
Roads into Taunton

The second toll-gate in Wellington erected in 1809 is also shown by Greenwood 1822 as 'T.B.' at the northern end of the main road through the town, at the junction with the old lane to Jurston Farm.

Toll-gates were universally disliked and in 1842 it was reported that the 'new' Wellington toll-gate had been thrown down with some violence. In 1851 the 'collector of tolls' was William Smith, living in the toll-house, between Little Jurston and Lodge House, with his wife Eliza, and their son and daughter.

Trull Toll-house
(approx ST 216229)
Roads into Taunton

The toll-gate from Shuttern toll-house which was by then in central Taunton was moved to Wild Oak Lane, Trull in 1851. The site was probably at the junction of Wild Oak Lane with the main road to Blagdon Hill (and eventually to the Devon border) originally turnpiked in 1752.

The 1871 Census places it between College Lodge and the Vicarage, Trull with 'toll gate keeper' David Leaver, aged 53, living there with his wife Elizabeth.

Chelston Toll-house
(approx ST 154211)
Roads into Taunton

The main road from Taunton (now B3187) went through the village of Chelston (Chilson on old maps) before entering Wellington.

The 1871 Census shows 'Turnpike Gate House Chelston' as being occupied by Betsey Crocker, aged 60, as 'toll collector', together with her daughter Mary and grand daughter Emma. It probably stood just outside of the village itself, but nothing remains today.

Bishop's Hull Toll-house
(approx ST 205248)
Roads into Taunton

Before the Wellington New Road was built in 1838/9, the old 1752 turnpike into Taunton from Wellington turned north at the crossroads near Stonegallows Inn and ran through Bishop's Hull, before going along Compass Hill to the end of Trull Road in Taunton.

The 1871 census places the toll-house between Long Run and Mount Street in Bishop's Hull but because of modern street names, it is not possible to determine exactly where in the village it stood. The 'toll collector' was David Hathway aged 57, living there with his wife Jane and two unmarried daughters.

Shuttern Toll-house, Taunton
ST 223242
Roads into Taunton

photo: janet dowding

The old 1752 turnpike via Bishop's Hull ran up Compass Hill to the end of Trull Road where Shuttern toll-house still stands although much altered and enlarged. It was originally erected in 1815 to replace a more modest house, which had probably been there since 1752.

Its size reflects the fact that it served as the meeting place of the Taunton Trustees and in 1845 it became the Taunton Eye Infirmary. The gate was removed in 1851 to Trull and in 1853 it was sold to James Billet for £400. The Infirmary closed in 1904, an old drawing of 1905 showing it then to have had two storeys, two projecting wings, Gothick windows and a crenellated roofline.

Handy Cross Toll-hut,
(ST 124314) **Lydeard St Lawrence**
Roads into Taunton

The road from Taunton (The Bridewell / Town Bridge) to Handy Cross was turnpiked in 1752 and the 1778 Act extended the turnpike from Handy Cross to Hartrow Gate (ST 091347). On the 1806 Trust map a toll-gate is shown just west of the Handy Cross junction, as well as a Bar one mile to the north-west.

The Trust minutes for 4 July 1854 record 'The Sentry Box lately provided by the Trustees for the collection of tolls at Handy Cross' had been destroyed by fire and a £10 reward offered.

Four Lost Taunton Toll-houses

Roads into Taunton

Frizehill Toll-house, Taunton
(ST 220255)   'T.G.' 'T.B.'
Roads into Taunton

The north-western entry to Taunton had a toll-house at Frizehill Gate, built around 1810 on the bend now just south of the railway bridge. Historical records are a little confused about many of Taunton's gates: in 1841 the George Inn Gate was removed to Frizehill and a new one erected at the Crown and Sceptre, whilst other records have Frizehill Gate not moved, but possibly replaced in 1861 by a gate at Cross Keys. The Census that year shows the 'collector of tolls' as 40 year old Simeon Bonning living there with his wife Cate.

Rowbarton Toll-house, Taunton
(ST 226256)
Roads into Taunton

The Rowbarton (or Kilkenny) Turnpike House had a salaried keeper paid £12 p.a. in 1752. It stood at the junction of present day Greenway Road (A358) and Kingston Road, one of the many toll-gates that once ringed old Taunton.

Thomas Manning, the keeper in 1758, was disciplined for misbehaviour. In 1832 the Rowbarton toll-gate was removed, but was reinstated in 1850. The 1851 Census has William Attwood, aged 50, as the 'toll collector' with his wife and two children there.

Holway Toll-house, Taunton
(ST 237235)
Roads into Taunton

Sited just north of Holway Avenue on the Taunton to Staple Fitzpaine road, in 1752 Holway toll-house had a salaried keeper earning £5 p.a. In the 1841 Census it was occupied by James Easton, a gardener.
During the 1840's efforts were made to sell Holway since a superior toll-house (presumably Silver Street) was acquired nearer the town centre. In 1860 it was finally resited at Pisces Bridge ST 237235 and was still functioning in 1871 when Mary Tamlyn aged 60 was 'toll collector'.

Spital Gate Toll-house, Taunton
(ST 239248)   'Toll'
Roads into Taunton

The first edition 1" OS map marks the site of Spital Gate as 'Toll' very close to the old Spital Almhouses at the junction of the old String Lane and Bridgwater Road (now Leycroft Road and Hamilton Road).
Although this gate was moved further out from the centre of the growing town of Taunton to Halcon Corner (ST 248248) in 1851, the toll-house continued in occupation at least until 1871 when the 'Old Toll House' was occupied by Alfred Balpin, a general dealer, and his wife Elizabeth, a glover.

Silver Street Toll-house, Taunton
ST 232243   'T.B.'
Roads into Taunton

photo: janet dowding

This rather odd looking building is believed to be the Silver Street Gate, known as 'Folly Toll House' in 1752 when it had a salaried keeper paid £12 p.a. According to historical records, the Silver Street Gate was re-erected in 1783 at New Cross Lane (now Holway Avenue), but there is a separate entry for 'Holway Lane Toll House' in 1752 and in the 1841 Census. In the latter John Rawlings aged 40 is shown as 'Gatekeeper' in Silver Street.

In November 1858 the surveyor of the Trust was ordered to cleanse and repair the cesspool at Silver Street Gate so as to procure a sufficient supply of water there! In 1871 'Silver Street Toll-Bar' was occupied by Lewis Delbridge aged 48, a 'Pensioner Royal Marines', his wife and four children

Lost Taunton Toll-houses

Taunton in the early days of the Trust was ringed by toll-houses, but when the town expanded in the 1840's and 1850's, some became too central and, after protests and complaints, were either abandoned, relocated or superseded by newer gates further out. Little is known about their exact locations, but they include North Town Toll-gate, Cockpit Gate near the Crown & Sceptre Inn, George Inn Gate and Newcastle Gate.

Some gates further out and known only from mentions in records include those at Blagdon, Stoke St. Gregory (Lyng Gate), Mere Elm, Pipers Inn (ST 441363), Kenny Gate (Ashill), Langford Bridge (ST 204263) and a side-bar at Langford Turn (ST 199268).

Lost Toll-houses east of Taunton

Roads into Taunton

Greinton Toll-house
(ST 403348)   'T.P.'
Roads into Taunton

The first edition 1" OS map shows a 'T.P.' at Greylake Fosse in the parish of Greinton, just north-east of Greylake Bridge over King's Sedgemoor Drain. Originally turnpiked by Wells Trust in 1779 this road was transferred to Taunton Trust in 1799, after which date the toll-house was probably built.

The 1871 Census records 'Turnpike Gate House' close to Greylake Foss Cottage and occupied by William Parsons aged 46, 'pensioner' with his wife Eliza. The house was sold in 1875 at the demise of the Trust.

Tuckers Gate Toll-house, Lyng
(approx ST 333288)
Roads into Taunton

In 1752 Taunton Trust extended only to Athelney Bridge (ST 347290), the remaining length to Piper's Inn being turnpiked by Wells Trust in 1779. 'Tuckers Gate' in the Parish of Lyng was transferred to Taunton Trust in 1799.

The 1871 Census places the toll-house near Vicarage House, which would be in East Lyng along with the church. Living in the toll-house in 1871 was Samuel Gillard aged 53, basket maker, with his wife Anna and six children.

Greylake Toll-house, Middlezoy
(ST 388336)   'T.B.'
Roads into Taunton

Greenwood's 1822 map shows a 'T.B.' at the junction of the present A361 with the minor road to Weston Zoyland, a short distance south of Kings Sedgemoor Drain in the hamlet of Greylake.

Known as Blindman's Gate, in 1871 'Turnpike Gate' was occupied by Thomas Reed aged 66, 'Turnpike Gate Keeper' and his wife Elizabeth. At the demise of the Trust in 1875, the toll-house was sold.

Burrowbridge Toll-house
(ST 357304)
Roads into Taunton

The toll-house at Burrowbridge is believed to have been erected between 1783 and 1809. In May 1799 the Taunton trustees ordered the road north of 'Burrow Bridge' to be 'formed and made' i.e. repaired, when they took it over from the Wells trust.
They also supported the 1824 Burrowbridge Act which made the bridge a 'Toll Bridge' under Bridge Commissioners. Tolls continued to be taken there right up to 1944 when the toll-gate was removed and the toll-house pulled down.
In 1871 the toll collector was Charles Goodson, aged 16, living there with his 21 year old brother James.

Walford Toll-house, now at Durston
(ST 276281) 'T.G.' 'T.B.' ST 291281
Roads into Taunton

photo: janet dowding

The Walford toll-house originally stood at the junction where the road from Exeter through Taunton split into branches to Bristol (A38) and Wells (A361), both turnpiked by Taunton Trust in 1752. The site is recorded on both the first edition 1" OS and Greenwood's maps.

The 1871 Census shows the 'Walford Creech St. Michael Toll House' as occupied by John Hayman aged 61, 'toll gate keeper' and his wife Sarah. When the old road from Monkton Elm to Walford Cross was dualled in the 1960's, the toll-house was relocated to Durston, the next village eastwards on the present A361. It survives today as a pretty cottage with leaded light windows and decorative barge-boards.

Wrantage Toll-house, North Curry
(approx ST 319230)
Roads into Taunton

The section of the present A378 from Mattock's Tree Green via Wrantage to Red Post, Fivehead, was turnpiked in 1752. The toll-house would have stood somewhere between the village of Wrantage and the turning to Rock village.

The 1871 Census places it on Wrantage Road so the site was probably at the junction with the side road to North Curry. In 1871 the 'Collector of turnpike tolls' was Ruth Humphrey aged 50 and unmarried. Nothing remains now.

Halcon Corner Toll-house, Taunton
ST 248249
Roads into Taunton

photo: janet dowding

The Old Spital toll-house was relocated to just west of Halcon Corner at ST 248248 in 1851 when most of the gates originally near the centre of town were moved further out. This was about a century after the road from Halcon Corner to Bathpool was originally turnpiked in the 1750's.

In 1871 the 'toll gate keeper' was George Pepler aged 55, living there with his 'Assistant' wife Edith and their daughter Mary. However in 1929 the toll-house was relocated again to a site in Bridgwater Road about 100 yards to the north-east. It survives today as 'The Old Turnpike', a lodge type house with mullioned windows and tiles with decorative fish scale bands.

Orchard Portman Toll-house
(ST 24?22?)
Roads into Taunton

The only evidence found so far for a toll-gate in the parish of Orchard Portman is from the 1851 Census which places it between 'Pickeridge' and 'Orchard Lane'. In 1851 it was occupied by William Francis aged 26, a mason, his wife Jane and their baby daughter Albena.

It is not known whether it stood on the present B3170 Taunton to Corfe road or the present unclassified road from Shoreditch to Staple Fitzpaine, the village of Orchard Portman being just south of the junction of these two roads.

Westhay Toll-house, Combe St Nicholas
ST 269125
Upottery - Ilminster

photo: janet dowding

Now known as 'The Old Toll House' and formerly 'Somersetshire Gate', this first toll-house north of the Devon border now stands on the A303, where the road from Bishopswood crosses towards Combe St Nicholas in the east. The original toll-house is the northern rounded part facing the road and now extended to the west it is one of very few thatched toll-houses remaining in Somerset.

The road here was originally built by the Honiton & Ilminster Trust, authorised in 1807 to run from the Honiton Turnpike at Upottery to Horton near Ilminster. The more easterly section from about a mile beyond Westhay was transferred to Ilminster Trust in 1829.

Brown Down Toll-house, Otterford
(approx ST 235133)
Upottery - Ilminster

The B3170 road north from the Devon border to Brown Down was turnpiked in 1828 by the Honiton & Ilminster Trust and its continuation to Corfe followed in 1840 by agreement with the Taunton Trust.

The 1841 Census for Otterford shows 'Brown Down Turnpike House' occupied by 'ag.lab' Samuel Hurford aged 71, but its exact position is difficult to determine other than somewhere between Brown Down Lane (ST 241122) and Waterhayes Lane (ST 233139). The 1861 Census calls it 'Old Turnpike House' so it may have ceased to function by then.

Lost Toll-houses, Churchingford

Roads into Honiton

Red Lane Toll-house,
(ST 203125)   **Churchstanton**
Roads into Honiton   'Toll'   'T.B.'

The first edition 1" OS map shows 'Toll' at Red Lane Crossroads west of the village of Churchingford. This is on the line of the 'Old Honiton Turnpike', of 1765, which ran from Honiton to Upottery and then into Somerset towards Taunton as far north as Trickey Warren and Glebe Farm and then on to Whitewall Corner after 1799.

On the map the toll-house appears to be on the north-west corner of the crossroads and therefore may not be the present day Red Lane Farm as is sometimes thought. Although the 'New Honiton Turnpike' was added after 1822 via Churchingford itself, this toll-gate continued to operate, the 'gate keeper' in 1871 being Mary Peters aged 27 living there with her 4 year old son John.

Churchingford Toll-house,
(ST 213126)   **Churchstanton**
Roads into Honiton

When the 'New Honiton Turnpike' was added in 1792 to join up with the Taunton turnpike, it ran from the Devon border through the village of Churchingford to Hunter's Lodge. A toll-house was obviously set up in the vicinity of the village itself because all four Censuses from 1841-1871 show 'gate keepers' there.

In 1851 the turnpike gate is shown as near the Royal Oak Inn and Mary Westcott aged 55 was the 'gate keeper', living there with her ag.lab husband Robert. It is not known whether an existing cottage in the village was used as the toll-house or whether one was specially built, as there is no obvious evidence either way.

Staple Fitzpaine Toll-gate
(ST 265182)
Roads into Taunton

The road from Taunton to Staple Fitzpaine was turnpiked in 1752, the trust's responsibility ending at Staple Pound which is shown on an 1806 trust map as immediately opposite the Greyhound Inn, in the north-west corner of the present crossroads.

However the trust map shows a toll-gate just south of the church at a now vanished road junction at ST 265182. Although shown on Taunton's plan, it may actually have belonged to Chard Trust which began at Staple Fitzpaine and ran southwards.

Snowdon Hill Toll-house, Chard
ST 312087   'T.Pike'   'T.B.'
Roads around Chard

photo: janet dowding

Although the roads here were originally turnpiked in 1777, this toll-house is believed to have been rebuilt in 1838 to take account of new gradients to the two routes it controlled, one west along the present day A30, the other south-west to Lower Wambrook.

Very much in the cottage ornée tradition with its 'gothick' pointed windows, flint façade, nail-studded door and overhanging thatched roof on posts, it is grade II listed and one of the most photographed in Somerset.

In 1871 the 'collector of tolls' was William Farracy aged 49 with his 'gate keeper' wife Fanny. The last occupant was Mrs. Nora Jewel who lived there for 75 years, well into the 20th Century.

Blackwater Toll-house
(ST 256154)
Roads around Chard

The Blackwater (or Blackdown) Gate House stood on the road from the hamlet of Holman Clavel south-eastwards into Chard, first turnpiked under the 1777 Act, disturnpiked in 1800 and eventually turnpiked again in 1830.

The toll-house is believed to have been built by William Bonfield of Crawley Foundry in 1854. The 1871 Census places it between Staple Hill Farm and the village of Blackwater; it was then occupied by Abraham Yard aged 40, his wife Caroline and their two children.

Crimchard Toll-house, Chard
ST 318094   'T.B.'
Roads around Chard

photo: janet dowding

On the 1777 turnpike road into Chard from Staple Fitzpaine, this is possibly an existing cottage adopted for toll-house use, rather than purpose built. In 1829 an income account stated £73 for this toll-gate, which caught traffic using Catchgate Lane just to the north, a short cut avoiding Snowdon Hill toll-house. An old picture shows it to have had a natural stone front with a central door and projecting porch roof.

In 1861 'Crimchard Turnpike Gate' was occupied by William Tizard aged 57, a 'Rural Postman and Toll Collector' along with his 'toll gate collector' wife Ann and two teenaged daughters. At the demise of the trust in 1875, George Masters was toll-collector and the property was auctioned to Edward Burrows.

Curland Toll-house
(ST 268174)   'T.B.'
Roads around Chard

Greenwood's 1822 map shows 'T.B.' at Bulford cross-roads, a mile south of Staple Fitzpaine (where the Chard and Taunton trusts met). The old road, first turnpiked in 1777, originally ran just east of Castle Neroche but was so steep and narrow that an easier route to the west was authorised in 1800 and completed in 1821.

An 1829 account for Curland Gate showed an income of £56. In 1841 Lord Portman 'required the removal of the stop gate at Staple' and a toll-house was finally built at Curland, which was repaired in 1854. In 1871 Charles Marshalsay aged 40 was 'Pensioner Sergeant and Gate Keeper' there.

Tytherleigh Toll-house (Devon)
(ST 318032)
Roads around Chard

photo: chard district museum

One of two toll-houses operated by the Chard Trust in Devon, Tytherleigh toll-house was just over the border on the Axminster road. A typical single storey building with 'gothick' pointed windows and door, it was like a stone and slate version of Snowdon Hill. Removed in the 1950's for road improvements, a grassy triangle now marks the site of the toll-house and its two gates, either side of which farmers having lands were exempt from tolls.

Thought to have been built by William Bonfield of Crawley Foundry in 1830, it stood at the junction with a side road to Broom. In October 1873 the tolls were auctioned for one year to the best bidder, and in 1875 at the demise of the Trust it was sold for £70 to a Mr. Langdon.

South Gate Toll-house, Chard
(ST 324083)
Roads around Chard

In 1829 the South Gate was erected near the King's Head Inn on the west side of Church Street, Chard, on the road towards Axminster (now A358), originally turnpiked in 1753.

In 1851 William Tizard (see Crimchard toll-house opposite) was 'Postman & Gate Keeper' there, with his wife Ann and four children. The toll-house was burnt down in 1857, but must have been rebuilt as at the demise of the trust, 'South Gate Toll House and gates' were Lot 6 in the auction on 22 December 1875 at the George Hotel, Chard and it was demolished some time later.

Windwhistle Toll-house, Cudworth
ST 383097   'T.B.'
Roads around Chard

photo: janet dowding

Standing next to the Windwhistle Inn, in an elevated position often enveloped by low cloud, this site is on one of the prehistoric trackways linking the North Dorset and Blackdown Ridgeways. Now the A30, the road was turnpiked in 1753. Little changed over the years except for its rear extension, Windwhistle toll-house still has its roadside porch tucked in next to the projecting gable end and in 1829 it made an income of £157.

In 1871 it was occupied by ag.lab Henry Bragg aged 30, his wife Jane and three children. On 22 December 1875 'the materials of the Windwhistle House, gates and posts' were sold at auction to Lord Bridport for £7, but it was not demolished for road widening as intended.

East Gate Toll-house, Chard
(ST 325086)
Roads around Chard

In 1830 East Gate was erected in East Street outside Chard School and in 1843 proposed alterations were estimated at £59 19s. 3d., an old plan showing a kitchen, pantry and two bedrooms over with 'gothick' windows.

In 1851 the mayor appealed for the removal of this unpopular gate because it was harming trade. It was relet in 1855 and a wooden replacement toll-house built there in 1857 burnt down a few months later. A temporary house was then built, only to be burnt again in 1862. Repairs costing £20 were made 'to make the ruins habitable' and despite further requests for its removal, it survived for a few more years.

Chard Borough Toll-house
ST 330097
Roads around Ilminster

photo: janet dowding

This building in Chard Borough is a possible toll-house, but on a turnpike road administered by the Ilminster Trust, turnpiked in 1759.

It stands at the junction of the present A358 and the side road to Chaffcombe, just north of Furnham where a toll-bar was set up in 1830 by the Furnham coal wharf. It is possible that this toll-house was built as a later result of this or even that Furnham toll-bar and this toll-house are one and the same.

In 1851 it was occupied by Richard Vincent, a 55 year old farmer, his housekeeper niece Caroline and his nephew Richard.

The Chard Trust: A Note

The history of roads around Chard is a little more complex than most, as the roads through both Crewkerne and Chard were first turnpiked under the 1753 act for roads around Yeovil, including a route right through to Axminster in Devon. Although the buildings are probably later, the sites of both Windwhistle and Tytherleigh toll-houses are on this original route.

The Chard Trust proper came into being when the act was renewed in 1777, adding in the road west from Chard to Cheeseway Ash (now A30) and the road to the south-east by-passing Chard, from White Down via Perry Street to the county boundary at Tytherleigh (now B3167).

Catherine Wheel Toll-house, Ashill
ST 334164
Roads around Ilminster

photo: janet dowding

The old road from Kenny Gate, on the Taunton side of Ashill, to the east end of Chard was turnpiked in 1759 and survives almost intact as the former A358. This toll-house stands at the north corner of the cross-roads at Catherine Wheel and was one of eight Ilminster Trust gates mentioned in a notice dated 6 October 1806, offering the tolls for auction. The 1840 survey of turnpike roads has 'toll' marked here.

Although small, in 1871 the toll-house accommodated 42 year old 'toll keeper' Harriott Hopkins, her labourer husband Walter and their seven children ranging in age from 1 to 17. At the demise of the trust this toll-house was conveyed by the Trustees to G.F. Speke in a document dated 11 December 1878.

Hornsbury Toll-house,
(ST 334108)   'T.B.'
Roads around Ilminster

About a mile north of Furnham, Greenwood's 1822 map shows a 'T.B.' in Hornsbury, near the Mill, at the junction of the Chard to Donyatt road, turnpiked in 1759, with a side road to Knowle St. Giles. It is one of the eight toll-gates of the Ilminster Trust for which the tolls were let by auction to the 'best bidder' on 1 November 1806.

In the 1871 Census, John Bush is shown as the 65 year old 'Gate Keeper and Toll Collector', living there with his wife Sarah and daughter Annie.

Horton Cross Toll-house
ST 339152
Roads around Ilminster

photo: janet dowding

Just east of Horton Cross, Ildene Cottage is grade II listed and may be the toll-house moved from its original position at Horton Cross (Horton Elm on the 1840 survey map). Here the 1759 Ashill to Chard road crossed the old A303 Honiton to Ilminster road.

Although described as a 'cottage ornée', the blind window over the blocked central doorway and the 'gothick' windows certainly suggest a toll-house. Originally 19th Century but altered and extended to the rear in the 20th Century, it is of local stone, rendered and colourwashed, and has a hipped clay plaintile roof and brick chimney stacks.

The 'gate keeper' in 1871 was William Smith aged 68, living there alone.

Cross Gate Toll-house, Ilminster
(ST 361142)   'T.B.'
Roads around Ilminster

Greenwood's 1822 map shows a 'T.B.' near the present Swanmead School and Cross Farm in Ditton Street, Ilminster, on the old 1759 turnpike road from Ilminster to Peasmarsh.

It is one of the eight toll-gates to be mentioned in a notice of 6 October 1806 notifying the auction of tolls on 1 November. The 1861 Census records Mary Goodrey Carter, aged 27 and unmarried, was 'Dressmaker and T. Pike Gate Keeper' there, with her 14 year old servant.

Hazelwell Toll-house, Ilminster
ST 347151
Roads around Ilminster

photo: janet dowding

A 1768 map of Ilminster shows the Hazelwell Turnpike Gate further east at ST 351150, near where the Chard Canal later crossed under the road. In 1842 the old toll-house was sold for £85, at which time the new toll-house was probably built. It is an imposing grade II listed building built of limestone under a slate roof, of two storeys with an off centre projecting bay, the front door now replaced by a window.

In 1851 James Trott aged 44 was the 'Turnpike Tolls Collector and Cordwainer' living there with his wife Sarah and son James. At the time of writing, the toll-house is sadly unoccupied, boarded up and for sale, needing comprehensive refurbishment.

Stocklinch Toll-house,
(ST 373177)
Roads around Ilminster

The 1845 Stocklinch Magdalen tithe map shows a toll-house and gate adjoining a junction on the 1759 turnpike road from Ilminster to Westport. This gate controlled the side road from Ilford Bridges to Bridge Cross, disturnpiked in 1803, never of much importance as most traffic on the main road was stopped at Old Way Gate just beyond Ilford Bridges.

In 1871 Stocklinch Gate was occupied by 'Toll Keeper' Susan Marshalsea aged 53, living there with her son and daughter. This side-gate survived until the trust was dissolved as in December 1878 the toll-house was sold to V.H. Vaughan Lee for £55.

Old Way Toll-house, Ilton
ST 365173
Roads around Ilminster

photo: janet dowding

The toll-house at Old Way Gate survives at the junction of the Ilminster to Westport road (B 3168) and the now minor road to Three Oaks Cross, the western section of the road from Three Oaks to Bridge Cross, South Petherton turnpiked in 1759. The original toll-house would appear to be the part facing the road and has obviously acquired a wing at the back at some later date.

Old Way is one of the eight gates mentioned in a notice of 6 October 1806 announcing the auction of tolls on 1 November to the 'best bidder'. In 1851 Alfred Walton, aged 47, was the 'Leastor (sic) of Turnpike' here and in 1871 Old Way Gate was occupied by 74 year old 'gate keeper' William Cossins, living there with his 65 year old wife Mary.

Ruskway Toll-house, Barrington
(ST 386184)
Roads around Ilminster

The village street of Barrington was turnpiked by the Ilminster Trust in 1823 together with Ruskway Lane as far north as Westport (on the present day B3168). A toll-house was built where these roads met at the western end of Barrington.

The 1871 Census, which records the toll-house as next to or near The Priory, shows 57 year old John Marshalsay as 'Toll Gate Keeper' there, with his 6 year old son Hector.

Townsend Toll-house, Ilminster
ST 368146   'T.B.'
Roads around Ilminster

photo: janet dowding

This grade II listed surviving toll-house is shown by Greenwood 1822 as 'T.B.' but it is not shown on the 1768 Ilminster map. It stands on the 1759 turnpike road through Ilminster to Whitelackington on the east side of Ilminster town.

It is of two storeys, built of rough Ham Hill stone with a slate roof and all windows have hollow-moulded stone mullions. It has been altered and extended in the 20th Century but apparently the interior retains something of its 19th Century character.

In 1861 the 'Turnpike Gate Keeper' was Samuel Marsh aged 62, living there with his wife Susan. Its present address is 'Toll House', 12 Bay Hill, Ilminster.

Whitelackington Toll-house
(ST 375151)
Roads around Ilminster

Somerset Historic Environment Record includes on a 1798 map of Common Fields a turnpike gate and toll-house on the old 1759 turnpike between Ilminster and Petherton Bridge, at a point south of Dillington Farm, where Long Ponds Copse meets the road at its north-western extremity.

This was once part of Ilminster Without parish but is now in Whitelackington. This gate was one of the 8 toll-gates mentioned in a notice of 6 October 1806 for the forthcoming auction of tolls on 1 November.

Kingstone Toll-house, Dowlish Wake
ST 376135 'T.B.'
Roads around Ilminster

photo: janet dowding

The toll-house at Kingstone Gate, now grade II listed, survives on the 1759 turnpike road south from Ilminster to the present A30 junction at Warren (Rayn) Hill. Greenwood's 1822 map shows it as 'T.B.'

Believed to have been built in the early 19th Century, it has been extended in the 20th, with the original door to the road now replaced by a casement window. It has a Welsh slate roof and is built of Ham stone rubble with ashlar dressings and mullioned windows on the road end.

In 1861 the 'gate keeper' was William Matthews aged 55, living there with his wife Jane. At the demise of the trust it was conveyed by the Trustees to William Speke in a document dated 11 December 1878.

Bridge Cross Toll-house,
(ST 447165) **South Petherton**
Roads around Ilminster

The Somerset Historic Environment Record includes a toll-house site at Bridge Cross on the old Ilminster to Yeovil road, turnpiked in 1759, now the A303. In 1822 Greenwood also recorded a toll-gate there. In a notice of 6 October 1806, Bridge Cross Gate was one of eight toll-gates of the Ilminster Trust for which the tolls were auctioned on 1 November.

In 1871 'Bridge Turnpike' was occupied by David Masters, a thatcher, aged 31, living there with his wife Sarah as 'Gate Keeper' and their four children. The toll-house has since been demolished.

73

OdcombeToll-house, Montacute
ST 501167 'T.B.'
Roads around Ilminster

photo: janet dowding

On Greenwood's 1822 map there is a 'T.B.' shown where this building now stands on the 1759 Ilminster to Yeovil road, at the junction of Yeovil Road and Woodhouse Lane.

It is unclear whether this building is the original toll-house, which would originally have had a doorway between the two lower windows. If it is, it has obviously been enlarged.

Odcombe Gate is another of the eight toll-gates mentioned in a notice of 6 October 1806, auctioning the tolls to the 'best bidder', the auction to take place on 1 November. In 1861 the 'toll collector' was Sarah Bird aged 66 and widowed, living there alone.

Roundham Toll-house
(ST 422098) 'T.B.'
Roads into Crewkerne

The road through Crewkerne from Roundham on the A30 to the west, via Maiden Beech Tree, to Misterton Cross on the A356, was turnpiked in 1765. The toll-house at Roundham stood just west of the village on the part of the A30 that originally belonged to the Yeovil / Chard Trust but was transferred to Crewkerne Trust in 1825. It is shown as 'T.B.' by Greenwood 1822.

In 1861 the 'Toll Gate Keeper' was Grace Hulford, aged 40, single and living there alone.

Clapton Toll-house
ST 420077
Roads into Crewkerne

photo: janet dowding

This small plain cottage is the Clapton Gate toll-house, situated on the B3165 south-west of Crewkerne, at the junction with the lane to Woolminstone, this road having been turnpiked in 1765.

Because it is close to the village of Hewish, it was known in the 1851 census as 'Clapton or Hewish Turnpike'.

In 1861 the 'Turnpike Gate Keeper' was Abel Marsh, living there with his wife Susan and four children. The toll-house still has a small roadside porch, which appears to be original.

Merriottsford Toll-house
(ST 443121)   'T.B.'
Roads into Crewkerne

Merriottsford toll-house once stood at 'Pyke Corner' as shown on the first edition 1" OS map, where Greenwood also shows a 'T.B.' in 1822. This is the junction of the Lopen Head to Broadshard road turnpiked in 1765, and the Merriott to Haselbury Bridge road turnpiked in 1825.

'Toll Gate House' was occupied in 1871 by James Beagley aged 44 as 'Toll Gate Keeper and Chelsea Pensioner', together with his wife Elisabeth and four children.

Misterton Toll-house
(ST 461079)   'T.G.'   'T.B.'
Roads into Crewkerne

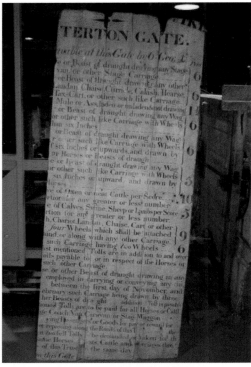

Just south-east of Misterton village is the crossroads of the present day A356 and A3066 where a turnpike gate and toll-house were sited by 1770. The two roads south of the cross-roads were turnpiked in 1765 and the A3066 northwards towards Grey Abbey in 1825. Greenwood's map for 1822 shows a 'T.B.' there and the first edition 1" OS map shows a building in the south-east corner of the crossroads.

In 1861 the toll-house was occupied by ag.lab Angel Paul, aged 60, and his wife Mary and daughter Charlotte. The toll-house survived until March 1935 when it was demolished. The toll-board however still survives and is in the County museum service's collection.

photo: somerset museum service

Bow Gate Toll-house, West Chinnock
(ST 458133)
Roads into Crewkerne

Bow Gate toll-house was situated on the present A356, turnpiked in 1765, at the junction with the road to West Chinnock, just south of Bow Mill. The first edition 1" OS map has the words 'Bow Gate' slightly to the north at ST 456134, where Eight Acre Hill toll-gate once stood (qv).

'Bow Turnpike' was occupied by John Marshallsay aged 36, shown as 'Gate Keeper' in the 1851 Census, living there with his wife Susan and four children. On modern maps 'Bow Gate' is still shown, but in the right place.

Shutteroaks Toll-house
ST 435109   'T.B.'
Roads into Crewkerne

photo: janet dowding

This toll-house, with its projecting porch and little side window for the better observation of traffic, appeared on the 1822 Greenwood map as 'T.B.' It stands beside Shutteroaks Bridge on one of Crewkerne's less important roads, that north-westwards to the village of Hinton St George, turnpiked in 1765.

This road was not made into a 'main road' when the new Highways Board took over the Trust roads and remains today a very narrow, steep and unimproved lane.

Now called 'Haunted House' the toll-house remains as 'Shutteroaks Toll House' on modern maps. In 1851 the 'Gate Keeper' was William Salisbury aged 30, living there with his wife and seven children.

Eight Acre Hill Toll-gate,
(ST 456134)   **West Chinnock**
Roads into Crewkerne

A toll-gate once stood at the junction of the present A356 (previously B3165) with the road to Boozer Pit, Merriott. This short stretch of road was turnpiked in 1825 and remained so until the demise of the trust in 1878, when it was not designated as a 'main road' by the new Highways Board.

Both modern maps and the 1841 Census call the site 'Hut Gate', but in 1871 it was 'Eight Acre Hill Gate' with Margaret Stower, a 74 year old widow living there as 'Gate Keeper' with her unmarried 33 year old daughter Martha Ann. This Census shows it to be positioned between 'Green Nap' and 'Bow Mills'.

Easthams Gate Toll-house
ST 456106 'T.G.'
Roads into Crewkerne

photo: janet dowding

Easthams Gate toll-house stands today on the A30 Yeovil Road about a mile out of Crewkerne, just before Haselbury Bridge. This originally Yeovil / Chard Trust road was transferred in 1825 to Crewkerne Trust, who in 1830 realigned the road to avoid the old Haselbury Bridge, and probably built the toll-house too.

It is of local Ham stone with a hipped Welsh slate roof, and has 'gothick' pointed windows and a blocked doorway facing the road.

In 1871 it was occupied by Mary Ann Whimpole, a 36 year old widow, as 'Toll Collector', with her 8 year old daughter. It is now used as a farmhouse and is grade II listed.

Haselbury Bridge Toll-house
(ST 459110) 'T.G.'
Roads into Crewkerne

A toll-house known as 'Haselbury Bridge Toll House' in 1841, 'Lower Gate, Haselbury' in 1851 and 'Severall's Gate' in 1871 stood close to Haselbury Bridge just south of Severall's Farm. The road that ran from Haselbury Bridge to Merriott was turnpiked in 1825, but the bridge was by-passed by the main road in 1830.

In 1871 the toll-house was occupied by 'Toll Gate Keeper' Mary Purchase, a widow aged 59, living there with her 7 year old grandson.

Norton sub Hamdon Toll-house
ST 463159
Roads into Crewkerne

photo: janet dowding

This now plain looking house would once have had a porch and toll-board recess on the front facing the road, but both are now blocked. It stands on the A356 (previously B3165) road from Crewkerne to Martock, turnpiked in 1765.

Isolated from Norton sub Hamdon village, at Turnpike Cross, the toll-house has been altered and added to in later years. It is of two storeys with a gabled pantile roof and walls mainly of squared local stone, with square headed casement windows.

The 1851 Census records George Rose, a widower aged 58, as 'Gate Keeper' living there alone.

Atkins Gate Toll-house, South
(ST 440178)   'T.B.'   **Petherton**
South Petherton - Martock - Somerton

A toll-house stood on the road from Martock to South Petherton, turnpiked in 1803, where the road to East Lambrook joined, scheduled to be turnpiked under the 1831 Act, but probably never actually done. The 1822 Greenwood map shows a 'T.B.' here whilst the first edition 1" OS map shows 'Atkins Gate' adjacent to the present Mill Lane.

In 1861 the toll-house was occupied by John Grinton, aged 70, living there as 'Gatekeeper' with his wife Susan. The location is still shown as 'Atkins Gate' on modern maps.

Lost Toll-houses near Martock

South Petherton - Martock - Somerton

Coat Toll-house, Martock
(ST 451202)   'T.B.'
S Petherton - Martock - Somerton

Coat toll-house was just west of Coat village, on the road north of Martock from Gawbridge Mill via Stapleton to Tintinhull. The mill was probably the chief economic reason for the survival of the turnpike road west of Stapleton, as beyond it the road was not successfully turnpiked.

The toll-house is believed to have been built by 1811 and the 1841 Census shows Joan Baker as 'Gate Keeper' there. It was still operating in 1861 when 38 year old cordwainer William Slade Horey was there with his son and daughter.

Bower Hinton Toll-gates
(approx ST 457179 & 458189)
S Petherton - Martock -Somerton

The 1871 Census includes entries for two separate turnpike gates in the village of Bower Hinton south of Martock. One toll-house was occupied by pensioner John Gibbs with his wife Harriet, aged 50, as 'toll collector', whilst the other was occupied by labourer James Whedon with his wife Martha, aged 49, as 'Gate Keeper'.
With nothing remaining of either, it can only be guessed that the toll-houses were at the junctions at either end of the village, the northern one known as 'Hurst Bow'.

Long Load Toll-house
(ST 467236 approx)
S Petherton - Martock - Somerton

The Victoria County History for Somerset records a turnpike gate towards the north end of Long Load village, erected by 1811, but it is not clear whether this had a toll-house attached. This road was turnpiked in 1761 as 'Dyed Way to Somerton'.

Stapleton Toll-house, Martock
(ST 463208)
S Petherton - Martock - Somerton

The Victoria County History records a toll-gate and cottage at a crossroads south of Long Load by 1815, presumably meaning Stapleton Cross.

It also states that the southern limit of the Load Tything (ST 462219) was marked by a crossroads called 'Yarley Nap' in 1811, formerly the site of a toll-gate. To confuse matters further, in 1822 Greenwood shows a toll-house at about ST 462200. It seems that the actual gate at Stapleton may have been moved several times.

The 1861 Census records 'Turnpike House' at Stapleton Cross with 38 year old ag.lab John Paul living there with his wife and daughter. There is no remaining evidence of any toll-house at any of the three possible locations.

West Gate Toll-house, Ilchester
(ST 521225)
Roads into Ilchester

photo: Ilchester museum

This toll-house stood at the western end of Ilchester on the old A303, originally turnpiked in 1753. It had no back garden, just a narrow side path to an equally small back yard, necessitating a trip down Pill Bridge Lane opposite every day with the 'night soil'. In 1861 it was occupied by 'Toll Collector' Charles Benfitt, aged 61, living there with his 11 year old son Charles.

An old photograph of 1920 shows Ilchester School built opposite it. Sometimes referred to as 'Mead Road Turnpike Cottage', another photograph of 1942 shows it still in existence then. It was finally demolished in 1964.

Cart Gate Toll-house
(ST 472182)
S Petherton - Martock - Somerton

The road from South Petherton via Martock to Cartgate was turnpiked in 1761. Cartgate itself marked the end of Martock Trust responsibility, north of where this road crosses the present A303, continuing on to Stoke sub Hamdon.

The 1861 Census records a toll-house at Cart Gate with 50 year old Susan Dymmock the 'Keeper of a Toll Gate' there along with her daughter and grandson.

Northover Toll-house, Ilchester
(ST 525232)
Roads into Ilchester

photo: ilchester museum

The Northover toll-house stood just north of Ilchester at the junction where the road from Exeter branched to Bristol and London. These roads were turnpiked in 1753, one later becoming the A37, the other the A303, both superseded by the Ilchester by-pass.

The toll-house was a plain rectangular cottage with the gable end facing the junction, probably originally with a porch over the door. In 1871 'Northover Turnpike Gate' was occupied by 51 year old 'Toll Gate Keeper' James Beckey.

Pulled down in 1959 for long needed road improvements, the wooden table of tolls for Northover Gate survives in Ilchester Museum.

South Gate Toll-house, Ilchester
(ST 523225)
Roads into Ilchester

South Gate toll-house stood on the old A37 (now B3151) road through Ilchester, where it heads south towards Yeovil, turnpiked in 1753. 'South Gate' and 'West Gate' derive from the gates of the once walled town, that dates back to Roman times.

The toll-house was just south of the junction with Almshouse Lane to the west and the road to Limington to the east. Anyone paying at Northover Gate could travel through South Gate without further payment. In 1871 the 'Turnpike Toll Collector' was James Farrow, aged 45, living there with his wife Eliza.

Sparkford Toll-house (The Octagon)
ST 607263　　'T.B.'
Roads into Ilchester

photo: janet dowding

It is not known for certain whether this early 19th Century grade II listed building is actually a restored large toll-house or a former drying house for the woollen industry, as suggested by one source.

Greenwood's 1822 map has a 'T.B.' here in Sparkford, on the old road from Petherton Bridge to Sparkford Bridge via Ilchester, turnpiked in 1792. The building could well be the toll-house as it stands close to the bridge where the trust's road ended.

Toll collectors are recorded in all four Censuses 1841-1871 living in Sparkford Road (now the Avenue). The last recorded 'Turnpike Gate Keeper' in 1871 was James Gale aged 67, living there with his wife Elizabeth.

> ## Sparkford Toll-gate
> (ST 605265)　　'T.B.'
> *Roads into Ilchester*
>
> On Greenwood's 1822 map there is a second 'T.B.' marked in Sparkford, this one on the present day A359, turnpiked in 1792, and probably close to where the Castle Cary Trust section of the A359 joined the Ilchester Trust section, now 'High Street'.
>
> Another source puts this toll-house further south-west near ST 602261. Wherever it stood, this toll house would have been short lived as in the Census years 1841-1871 there are no toll collectors recorded here.

Mudford Lane Toll-house, Yeovil
ST 558177
Roads around Yeovil

photo: janet dowding

Built around 1850, this grade II listed toll-house survives on the corner of St. Michael's Avenue and the main A359, originally turnpiked in 1753 as far as Mudford Bridge. Of local stone with a clay plaintiled roof with fish-scale bands and mullioned windows, the original door has been replaced with a 20th Century bay window.

Also known as Brickyard Lane toll-house, it is said to have replaced an earlier one closer to town where it served the dual purpose of stockyard gate to the nearby brickworks.

In 1861 'Mudford Lane Gate' was occupied by Joseph Jones aged 38, a licensed hawker with his 'Toll Collector' wife Mary and their two children. The toll-house was sold off in 1875.

Combe Street Toll-house, Yeovil
(ST 555177)   'T.B.'
Roads around Yeovil

Combe Street toll-house stood on the south side of Combe Street Lane, a short distance west of the junction with Mudford Road (A359). It was a side-gate only and appeared on Greenwood's 1822 map as 'T.B.' and on the tithe map as 'Hutt Gate'.

In 1851 Elizabeth Ellis aged 50, a glover, was living there and by 1861 it was known as 'Combe Street Gate' and occupied by Robert G. Shadforth, a coachmaker. These two may have also collected the tolls there or it may have ceased to function as a toll-house by then, as it was sold in 1867.

Kingston Toll-house, Yeovil
(ST 554165)
Roads around Yeovil

photo: source not known

The tithe map shows Kingston toll-house on the east side of the junction (now a roundabout) of Mudford Road (A359) with Ilchester Road (A37). Old illustrations show it as a quite large two storey building with decorative barge-boards over the projecting gable with a ground floor bay window.

In 1861 John Channing aged 47 was the 'Toll Gate Keeper', living there with his wife and daughter. At the demise of the trust in 1875 the gates across the road at the five crossways were removed and the site was sold. The toll-house was taken down and rebuilt a short distance closer to the town, but later in 1969 it was demolished for road widening and the site is now covered by Yeovil District Hospital.

Hendford Hill Toll-house, Yeovil
(ST 553155)
Roads around Yeovil

Hendford Hill toll-house was one of three 'capital gates' ordered to be built in 1753 by the Turnpike Commissioners. This one 'at Hendford Bridge, at or near the crossways on the north side of the turnpike road', is now the site of a large roundabout.

The toll-keepers at these gates received a salary of 6 shillings per week (8 shillings until the toll-house was completed). In 1851 the 'Turnpike Gate Keeper' was Joseph Warr aged 50, living there with his wife Jane. The toll-house was sold in 1875 and later demolished.

Penstile Toll-house, Yeovil
ST 562160
Roads around Yeovil

photo: janet dowding

This small grade II listed toll-house, similar to that in Mudford Road (qv) was originally at Coldharbour in the parish of Yeovil, on the corner of London Road and Newton Road. One storey with Ham stone ashlar dressings and a Welsh slate roof, it has an angled bay window with stone mullions. Built around 1850 it has a later two storey extension.

The 1841 Census records it as 'Penstile Gate on London Road' and in 1871 16 year old John Bunter was 'Turnpike Gate Keeper' there. In 1873 the site was sold, the house having been taken down in 1870 and rebuilt nearby on the corner of Newton Road and South Terrace. Sold in 1874, it survives as 'Newton Lodge', 22 Newton Road, Yeovil.

Goar Knap Toll-house, Yeovil
(ST 565164)
Roads around Yeovil

Another of Yeovil's three 'capital gates', the other two being Hendford Bridge and Head of Kingston, that at Goar Knap probably stood at ST 565164. This is the junction of Sherborne Road and St. Michael's Avenue, where a 'T.G.' was shown on the map produced for the 1840 Parliamentary Return of Turnpikes.

This gate operated until at least 1861 as shown by successive Census returns. At this date 'Goar Knap Turnpike Gate' was operated by 'Gatekeeper' Frances Hicks aged 48 living there with her husband Robert, a carter.

Yeovil Bridge Toll-house, Bradford Abbas (Dorset)
ST 574160
Roads around Yeovil

photo: janet dowding

This substantial Victorian toll-house survives little changed on the east side of Yeovil Bridge just into Dorset. It controlled the Yeovil Trust's road eastwards to Halfway House near Nether Compton, midway between Yeovil and Sherborne. Originally turnpiked in 1753, Babylon Hill east of the toll-house, now the A30, was improved in 1827.

The two storey toll-house is grade II listed with mullioned windows with latticed lights and has a plaintile roof with ornamental banding and a projecting bay to the front. In 1861 Benjamin Hurlstone aged 57 was 'Toll Gate Keeper', living there with his wife Mary and 2 year old grand-daughter Mary.

Foxwell Toll-house, East Chinnock
(ST 477123)
Roads around Yeovil

An old map of Yeovil Trust's roads shows a toll-gate (T.G.) at Foxwell Lane, between Haselbury Plucknett and East Chinnock, on the 1753 turnpike between Yeovil and Crewkerne. About six miles from Yeovil, it required a separate toll to be paid there, as no other gate 'cleared' this one.

Under the Yeovil and Ilchester Roads Act of 1852, it states "...A clause be inserted, directing the removal of the toll-gate at Foxwell Lane, immediately after the passing of the Act, this meeting being of opinion that the existence of such gate is a heavy and unnecessary burden upon persons travelling that line of road".

Closworth Toll-house
ST 564114
Barwick - Charminster etc.

photo: shirley melligan

The Maiden Newton Trust of Dorset had its two northernmost miles of road in Somerset, south of Whistle Bridge near Barwick. Closworth toll-house survives a quarter mile north of Prowle's Cross on the west side of the A37, originally turnpiked in 1778. Now enlarged, the original part of the toll-house is the small projecting bay with the door blocked and a central window over.

A prime example of toll-gates being operated by lone women without husbands to help, it was recorded as Prowle's Gate in the 1841 Census, with Mary Lanning aged 35 'Toll Keeper' there with her two children. In 1851 Catherine Larcombe aged 37 was 'Gate Keeper' (again with two children).

Whistle Bridge Toll-house, Barwick
(ST 562122)   'T.B.'
Roads around Yeovil

The A37 south of Yeovil largely follows the line of the Roman Ilchester to Dorchester road, the section to Whistle Bridge originally turnpiked in 1753 by the Yeovil Trust, but much of the present A37 was authorised by the joint Yeovil / Ilchester Act of 1852.

In 1851 'Whistle Gate', east of the road, was occupied by 'Turnpike Gate Keeper' James Beckey aged 51. The toll-house was sold in 1867 and by 1871 it was known as 'Whistle Bridge Old Turnpike Cott.', obviously having ceased to function. It was occupied by 47 year old widower and 'Marine Store Dealer' Elias Budgell with his family.

South Cheriton Toll-house, Horsington
ST 692248
Blandford - Bratton

photos: janet dowding

In the Vale of Blackmoor, another Dorset trust had roads into Somerset, this one covering about six miles of the present day A357 up as far as Lattiford, just south of Wincanton. The turnpiking of this road was included in the 1765 Act but may not have been completed until a later date.

This grade II listed toll-house survives at South Cheriton, the only one in Somerset with its toll-board of charges in situ (dated 19 July 1824). The toll-house is of stone with ashlar dressings and has a clay plaintile roof, 2-light chamfered mullioned windows and the original central canopied doorway.

In 1871 'Horsington Turnpike Gate' was occupied by 'Gate Keeper' Samuel Pike aged 28, living there with his wife Esther and daughter Kate.

Yenston Toll-gate, Templecombe
(approx ST 715212)
Blandford - Bratton

The Horsington Turnpike Gate's toll-board (above) is the only clue to the existence of a toll-gate at or near the village of Yenston about two miles north of the Dorset border, part of that county's Vale of Blackmoor Trust.

With no evidence coming to light so far of anyone living there, the actual position of Yenston Gate is not known and it might only have been a 'stop gate' without its own toll-house.

Bow Bridge Toll-house, Henstridge
ST 745213   'T.G.'
Sherborne - Shaftesbury

photo: janet dowding

Just on the Somerset side of the Dorset border, at the junction with a side road leading to Henstridge Marsh, the Bow Bridge toll-house survives on the south side of the present day A30, which from Milborne Port to Bow Bridge was turnpiked in 1753.

With its doorway blocked in and modern windows inserted, it is now mainly recognisable by the stone built canted bay front, facing the road. It has a clay plaintile roof and has been enlarged considerably in recent times.

In 1861 the 'Toll Collector' was 43 year old George Sweetman, living there with his wife Elizabeth and their five children.

Meadcombe Toll-house, Castle Cary
(ST 647311) 'T.B.'
Sherborne - Shaftesbury

An old road south of Ansford (Castle Cary) towards Sherborne crossed the present day A359 Sparkford to Bruton road at Meadcombe, where Greenwood (1822) shows a 'T.B.' To the south of this former crossroads there remains a footpath, but to the north the road was realigned along an upgraded lane to cross the main road further east at ST 651311.

The Meadcombe toll-house must have gone out of use soon after 1822, as the new layout is shown in 1828 on a Bruton Trust survey. It was also very near Smallway toll-house (qv), about half a mile to the south-west.

Green Lane Toll-house, Bratton Seymour
ST 666295
Sherborne - Shaftesbury

photo: janet dowding

Just off the present day A371, this toll-house survives on the old line of the 1753 turnpike road from Ansford Hill (Castle Cary) to Sherborne. At a junction with a short road to the west, which was never turnpiked, it is just south of Hix's Mead at the southern end of Cattle Hill.

Now known as 'The Old Toll House' the grade II listed building with several 20th Century extensions is built of stone with a clay plaintile roof. It has a canted projecting bay with the original doorway and toll-board recess now filled by windows.

In 1861, 66 year old Daniel Hill was 'Turnpike Gate Keeper, Toll Collector and Greenwich Pensioner', living there with Thomassin, the 'Collector's wife'.

Cattle Hill Toll-house, Bratton
(ST 667297)   **Seymour**
Sherborne - Shaftesbury

Also known as 'Sherborne Turnpike Cross Gate on Cattle Hill', Cattle Hill Turnpike Gate is shown on an 1827 turnpike plan just north of the A371 at what is now Hix's Mead, where roads from Sherborne, Bruton and Wincanton all met.

In 1830, the old and difficult roads through the grounds of Hadspen House were replaced by what is now the A371 to the west (for Castle Cary) and Cattle Hill to the north (for Bruton). It therefore seems likely that Green Lane Gate superseded Cattle Hill Gate at about this time.

Lost Toll-houses West of Wincanton

Sherborne - Shaftesbury

Roads around Wincanton

Grove Gate Toll-house, Hadspen
(ST 661306)   'T.B.'
Sherborne - Shaftesbury

About a mile north-west of Green Lane, Greenwood's 1822 map shows a 'T.B.' on the turnpike road from Sherborne in Dorset which came up into Somerset as far as Ansford. The toll-house stood near the entrance to Hadspen House on the present A371.

Census entries show it was operating between 1841 and 1871, somewhere between Shatwell Farm House and Grove Farm. At the latter date the 'Gate Keeper' was 30 year old Jane Harris, living there with her ag.lab husband William and their 5 children.

Cuddlescomb Toll-house,
(ST 678292)   **Bratton Seymour**
Roads around Wincanton

A toll-house called 'Cuddlescomb Gate' is shown on the Census returns for 1851, 1861 and 1871 not far from Green Lane Gate. It probably stood a little further east along the present day A371, originally turnpiked in 1756, at the junction now called 'Jack White's Gibbet', at the top of a valley leading down to Cuttlesham Farm.

In 1861 the 'Turnpike Gate Keeper or Toll Collector' was George Mitchell aged 66, living there with his wife Elizabeth.

South Cadbury Toll-house
(ST 631263)
Roads around Wincanton

The old road from Sparkford Bridge to Bourton on the Dorset boundary was turnpiked in 1756. The South Cadbury toll-house probably stood at 'Chapel Cross' where the road between North Cadbury and South Cadbury crossed it. The whole junction there has now been incorporated into the new A303 trunk road set up.

The toll-house survived until at least 1861, when it was occupied by George Stone aged 57, a 'Pensioner', and his wife Jane. Either he collected the tolls there or possibly the toll-house had ceased to function by then.

Abergavenny Toll-house,
(ST 701285)   **Wincanton**
Roads around Wincanton

Also known as 'West Gate Turnpike House', the Abergavenny toll-house stood on the old route of the A371 from Bratton Seymour into Wincanton, turnpiked in 1756. East of Holbrook House Hotel this old road is now unclassified. In 1791 this toll-house made a profit of £45 19s. 2d. i.e. what was left after deducting labour, maintenance and collection costs from the tolls received.
In 1871 the 'Toll Collector' was Mary Davidge, a widow aged 34, living there with her two young children.

East Gate Toll-house, Wincanton
ST 717287
Roads around Wincanton

photo: janet dowding

Now grade II listed and known as 'The Old Toll House', Wincanton's East Gate survives on the corner of High Street and Common Road, each of which had a gate. The former A303 through the town was part of the original 1756 road from Sparkford Bridge to Bourton on the Dorset boundary and this gate is believed to have been set up in 1791, when it produced a profit of £131 3s. 10d.

The building probably dates from then and appears in old photos with a canted bay with 'gothick' windows and a hipped roof. In 1874 when the gates were removed, this was cut back to a gable with a decorative bargeboard. In 1851 it was occupied by 33 year old 'Shoemaker and Turnpike Gate Keeper' James Cox and his wife Emma and their two children.

South Gate Toll-house,
(ST 710281)   **Wincanton**
Roads around Wincanton

Wincanton's 'South Gate' stood east of Hawker's Bridge on the south side of what is now Southgate Road. Its 1791 profit was £146 9s. 2d. An old photograph shows the gate adjacent to a row of cottages, one of which might possibly have served as the toll-house. 'South Gate Cottages' there now appear to be a later Victorian rebuild.

Referred to as 'Tything' in the Census, in 1871 'Sth Toll Gate' was occupied by 'Toll Collector' Mary Hannam aged 54, living there with her husband, a Chelsea Pensioner, her 10 year old daughter, and her unmarried brother Charles.

Lost Toll-houses East of Wincanton

Roads around Wincanton

Stoney Stoke Toll-house
(ST 712319)
Roads around Wincanton

Under the note for the 1798 Act, accompanying the map of the Wincanton Trust's turnpike roads for the Parliamentary returns in 1840, there is mention of an 'Old Turnpike House' at Stoney Stoke. That it had gone by that date is confirmed by lack of evidence in any subsequent Census entries (1841 onwards).

It stood in the north-east corner of the junction leading to Charlton Musgrove off the Wincanton to Bruton road, these roads having been turnpiked by both Wincanton and Bruton trusts at various dates.

Southmarsh Toll-house
(ST 734308)　　　'T.B.'
Roads around Wincanton

Greenwood's 1822 map shows a 'T.B.' near Southmarsh and Ball Common, on what is now the B3081 between Stoney Stoke and Leigh Common (A303), turnpiked in 1818 and part of the route from Bruton to Gillingham in Dorset.

Nothing further is known of this toll-house except that in 1871 the 'Toll Collector' was 31 year old Ellen Bateman, living there with her 'Blacksmith, Journeyman' husband John and their 9 year old son Sidney.

Norton Ferris Toll-house
(ST 794371) 'T.B.' 'T.Pike'
Roads around Wincanton

Now in Wiltshire, the village of Norton Ferris was in Somerset until 1896 and the road through from Stourton to Maiden Bradley was turnpiked in 1798 by the Wincanton Trust.

Their toll-house was just north-east of the village south of the hill called Long Knoll and was shown on both Greenwood's 1822 map and the first edition 1" OS map. Census entries show it was certainly in operation in 1841, 1851 and 1861. At the last date, the 'Toll Collector' was Charlotte Holbrook aged about 21, living there with her 'Road Labourer' husband Alfred, who may also have worked for the Turnpike Trustees.

Mapperton Toll-house
(ST 782382)　　　'T.B.'
Roads into Bruton

Also shown on Greenwood's 1822 map there is another 'T.B.' in the 'Norton Ferrars Hundred'.

It stood on the Bruton to Maiden Bradley road, turnpiked in 1793, and the stretch north and east of where the toll-gate was (now Bradley Lane) may possibly have been built as a turnpike diversion to avoid Mapperton Hill. This road is shown on the 1828 Trust survey.

Nunney Catch Toll-house
(ST 739448)   'T.B.'   'T.P.'
Roads into Bruton

photo: courtesy d burry

Shown as 'Nunnery Ketch T.B.' on Greenwood's 1822 map, Nunney Catch toll-house stood in the angle on the west side of the junction where the old A359 headed south off the old A361, the site now isolated and disused due to the realignment of the A361 further south. The Leighton to Frome road (now A361) was turnpiked in 1756 by the Bruton Trust, but the A359 was not turnpiked through to Nunney Catch until 1810.

In 1851 Nunney Catch toll-house was occupied by 22 year old 'Toll Collector' Robert Hewlett, living there with 4 lodgers including a musician and an ostler. The toll-house was sold off for £80 in 1876 to Sam Charlton. It survived until its demolition in 1929/30 and the site is now occupied by a motor company.

Marston Gate Toll-house, Frome
(ST 765463)   'T.Pike'
Roads into Bruton

Both Greenwood's 1822 map and modern maps show 'Marston Gate' at the junction of the present Marston Road (B3090) and Marston Lane. Both roads go into Frome and, past the toll-house, the Bruton Turnpike continued to link up with Christchurch Street near the site of the old Lamb Inn (ST 776477).

In 1851 'Marston Gate' was occupied by 64 year old Richard Babey, listed as 'Colour Sergeant in the Army, Chelsea Pensioner and Toll Gate Keeper', together with his wife Alice, two daughters and a son.

Lost Toll-houses around Nunney

Roads into Bruton

Hartgill Toll-house, Nunney
(ST 723450) 'T.B.' 'T.Pike'
Roads into Bruton

The now vanished toll-house at Hartgill appeared in four separate publications: Greenwood's 1822 map, the first edition 1" OS map, the 1828 Bruton Trust survey and the 1830 Deposited Plan. It stood on the north corner of a small triangle of roads, with gates across the roads north to Whatley and Mells, turnpiked in 1793, and east into Nunney (the western end of Horn Street) turnpiked in 1810. Just south of the toll-house junction was the junction with the old A361, now diverted even further south.

In 1871 'Hartgill Toll Gate House' was occupied by 'ag.lab' Henry Phillips, aged 28, who presumably also took the tolls, and his wife Harriet and three children. The toll-house was sold off for £25 in 1876 to James Theobald, of a local wealthy family.

Nunney Gate Toll-house
(ST 735456)
Roads into Bruton

According to a local history of Nunney, there were 5 toll-gates in this parish, one of which was 'on the Castle Hill side of The Bellhouse', i.e. where Castle Hill and Horn Street meet. The road from Nunney Catch northwards through the village was turnpiked in 1793 by the Bruton Trust.

The toll-gate was certainly in operation in 1861, and in 1871 the toll-house was occupied by the four Budgett sisters, aged from 12 to 21. The eldest was Sarah who was the 'Toll Gate Keeper' in what was then known as 'Nunney Toll Gate House'.

Holwell Toll-house, Nunney
(approx ST 728449)
Roads into Bruton

The Holwell toll-house, also known as the 'Shepton Road Turnpike House', stood near Holwell Bridge on the old Leighton to Frome road through Nunney Catch, turnpiked in 1756. The present day A361 now by-passes this old stretch of road. The gate was actually only a side bar but was operating in 1841 when 60 year old Robert Uphill was 'Gate Keeper' there.

In 1851 it was occupied by William Dimmick aged 73, a 'pauper and Discharged Marine' and in 1861 by Betty Bradden aged 72, a widow and 'Arms Woman'. They may have collected tolls but by 1871 it was uninhabited. In 1876 it was sold off, only £1 being offered for it by James Gunning, but the turnpike minutes do not state whether this was accepted.

Bridge Toll-house, Nunney
ST 736456
Roads into Bruton

photo: janet dowding

This little building known as 'The Beehive' is the only thatched cottage left in Nunney and said to be one of the five toll-gates in the parish, so positioned that whichever way you went out of the village you paid tolls!

It stands on the corner of Market Place and Church Street (Frome Road), next to the bridge in the middle of the village. The north / south road here was turnpiked in 1793 and the east / west road in 1810 as far as Nunney Church, where the Frome Trust took over.

Also known (in 1871) as 'Toll Cottage, Frome Road', 'Bridge Gate' was occupied in 1851 by 26 year old John Hillier, 'ag.lab & Gate Keeper Toll', together with his wife Sarah and 3 young sons. It was sold off for £25 in 1876 to James Theobald.

Leighton Toll-house
(ST 701436) 'T.B.' 'T.P.'
Roads into Bruton

The Leighton toll-house stood at the northern end of the 1756 turnpike road from Bruton via Batcombe to Leighton where it joined the present A361 (the old junction has now been obliterated by realignment of the main road).

In 1861 'Leighton Toll Bar' was occupied by Richard Chappel aged 33, a 'Cordwainer and Collector of Tolls'. The Leighton toll-house was demolished some time after 1971, when it was recorded as 'of uncoursed limestone, part cement, rendered, roof stone, unoccupied and derelict'.

Lost Toll-houses near Bruton

Roads into Bruton

Mitchell's Elm Toll-gate,
(ST 696425)   'T.B.'   **Wanstrow**
Roads into Bruton

About a mile south of Leighton, Greenwood's 1822 map shows a toll-gate on the original 1756 turnpike route from Bruton to Leighton. Also known as Mitchell's Ash Gate, it was at the junction with Withy Wood Lane, the road west to Cranmore, which along with the section eastwards via Weston Town to Wanstrow, was disturnpiked in 1831 as it carried little traffic.

If there had been a toll-house here it was short-lived as the section of road from Batcombe to Leighton was also abandoned in 1867 and no evidence of this gate has yet been found in the Census entries.

Wanstrow Toll-house
(ST 712417)
Roads into Bruton

The main A359 was turnpiked in 1810 through to Nunney Catch, which involved building a completely new two mile section of road with Wanstrow village at its centre. The Wanstrow toll-house stood on the south-west corner of the village cross-roads, with 'Wanstrow Gate' across the main road and 'Wanstrow Side Gate' across Church Street. A third gate was later erected on Wanstrow Common but only operated for a number of years.

In 1871 the 'Toll Collector' was 21 year old Emma James and the toll-gate on the Common was operated by Joseph Seviour's family. In 1876 the Wanstrow toll-house was sold for £40 to Benjamin Giles who owned Arden Cottage, in the grounds of which the toll-house had been built.

Yarnfield Toll-house,
(ST 768376)   'T.B.'   'T.Pike'
Roads into Bruton

The first edition 1" OS map shows 'Yarnfield T.Pike' where the road from Bruton via North Brewham joins the road from Kilmington to Gare Hill, not turnpiked until 1793. Greenwood's 1822 map also shows a 'T.B.' there.

In 1851, 47 year old 'Toll Collector' Charles Hill was living there with his children William and Jane, who in 1861 appear living with their mother Ann Hill at West End toll-house, Bruton (qv).

When the Bruton Trust was wound up in September 1876, the newly formed Wincanton Highway Board ordered a road to be formed 'on the site of the old Tollhouse'. 'Yarnfield Gate' still appears on modern maps.

Burrowfield Toll-house, Bruton
ST 687351   'T.Pike'
Roads into Bruton

photo: janet dowding

Shown as 'Barrowfield T.Pike' on the first edition 1" OS map, this grade II listed toll-house survives at the east end of Bruton. It is at the junction of Brewham Road, the original 1793 turnpike to Maiden Bradley and beyond, and Frome Road (A359), a later branch to Nunney Catch turnpiked in 1810.

Probably built soon after this, the toll-house is a picturesque building with ornamental barge-boards to its gabled clay plaintile roof. It retains a porch on the north-west side, but that to the south-west has disappeared, along with the toll-board recess, now blanked out.

In 1871 the 'Toll Collector' was Isaac Bond, a 48 year old widower, living there with his son and two daughters.

Redlynch Toll-house
(ST 703334)   'T.P.'
Roads into Bruton

Two miles south-east of Bruton there was a toll-house at 'Redlynch Cross', on the Stoney Stoke road. This was turnpiked in 1756, as was the road that crossed here from Whatcombe Bottom (A359) to the White Horse in Hardway, an ancient route in decline by 1750. The section from the toll-gate eastwards to Hardway was disturnpiked in 1831, as shown on the 1840 Parliamentary Return map.

In 1871 the 'Turnpike Toll Collector' was 65 year old Ann Hill, there with her daughter Jane aged 26. The Hill family served the Turnpike for 20 years in 3 other Bruton toll-houses: Yarnfield, West End, and Lusty.

More Lost Toll-houses near Bruton

Roads into Bruton

Creech Hill Toll-house,
(ST 673363) 'T.P.' **Lamyatt**
Roads into Bruton

Shown as 'T.P.' on the first edition 1" OS map, Creech Hill toll-house stood about a mile out of Bruton on the west side of Creech Hill, just past the junction with Creech Hill Lane, leading back to Wyke Champflower, close to Lamyatt Beacon. This road from Bruton to Milton Bridge and beyond was turnpiked in 1756 and is now the B3081.

This toll-house was still in operation in 1871 when 'Creech Hill Gate House' was occupied by 'Gatekeeper' Harriott Field aged 47 living there with her labourer husband Frederick and their son and daughter.

Hedgestocks Toll-house, Batcombe
(ST 683373) 'T.Pike' 'T.B.'
Roads into Bruton

A toll-house shown on the early OS as 'Hedgestock T.Pike' stood at a cross-roads about two miles north of Bruton on the Leighton road, the original 1756 turnpike to Frome. The west-east road here from Milton Clevedon (B3081) to Copplesbury Farm (A359) was turnpiked in 1810 and probably disturnpiked by 1831, as it is not shown on the 1840 Parliamentary Return map. An 1828 survey shows the toll-house in the north-east corner of the crossroads with gates to both roads. It was still operational in 1861 when Elizabeth Padfield aged 41 was 'Toll Collector'.

The toll-board survived for some years in the Ward Library, Bruton, but its present whereabouts are unknown. In addition to the charges, it said that "a ticket taken at this gate clears the next gate passed through on the Bruton Trust".

Coombe Hill Toll-house
(ST 684352) 'T.G.'
Roads into Bruton

According to an old history of Bruton, the trust also had toll-gates called 'Sheepsleigh Gate' (whereabouts unknown) and 'Horningsham Gate', believed to have stood east of the Wiltshire village at ST 833406, where the early OS shows 'T.Pike'. This road was turnpiked in 1793.

The same map shows a 'T.G.' north of Bruton at Coombe Hill (ST 684352), where the unclassified road to Batcombe, part of the original 1756 turnpike to Frome, branches off the B3081 Bruton to Milton Bridge road. This was either just a 'stop gate' or an early short-lived toll-house as nothing further is known of it, not even in the Census returns of 1841-71 for this area.

West End Toll-house, Bruton
ST 679347
Roads into Bruton

photo: janet dowding

Now called 'Turnpike Cottage', this surviving toll-house stands at the junction of Bruton High Street and Shute Lane, part of the old road to Wyke Champflower. This road was the last to be turnpiked by the Bruton Trust in 1793.

An old photograph shows West End toll-house as a very small cottage with a porch on the front, side windows, a window above the porch in the gable and a very tall chimney. It has obviously been altered and extended over the years.

In 1861 'West End Turnpike Gate' was occupied by 'Toll Collector' Ann Hill, aged 55, living there with her unmarried son William and daughter Jane.

Lusty Toll-house, Bruton
(ST 679343)   'T.P.'
Roads into Bruton

Shown as 'Lusty Gate' on a turnpike map of 1824, a toll-house once stood on the A359 just south-west of Bruton. It was beyond the present railway bridge on the north side of Cole Road before the junction with Gants Mill Lane. This road was turnpiked in 1793 and although tortuous and hilly, it was the only reasonable route westwards from Bruton.

In 1861 the 'Turnpike Toll Collector' was William Keech aged 49, living there with his daughter and son. In 1871 it was occupied by Charles Hill, the father of the Hill family who occupied four different Bruton toll-houses over 20 years.

Smallway Toll-house, Castle Cary
(ST 640305)   'T.B.'
Langport - Somerton - Castle Cary

photo: castle cary living history group

A 'T.B.' is shown on Greenwood's 1822 map at the cross-roads of Smallway Lane and Galhampton Hill on the A359, turnpiked in 1792. Trust maps describe it as 'Hadspen Gate' in 1830 and 'Smallway Gate' in 1857. This old photograph taken on the road between Abbey and Smallway, reputedly shows the Smallway toll-house, but might be the (old) 'Galhampton Gate'.

Census returns show Smallway was operating in 1841 with 'Gate keeper' Matthew Gooden aged 15 (son of Robert Gooden of 'old' Galhampton Gate) and in 1871 when 'Smallway Turnpike House' was occupied by 'Gate Keeper' George Cooper, aged 68, and his wife Eliza. It was demolished in the 1960's when it was owned by Henry S. Perrot.

Shepherd's Cross Toll-house
(ST 637310)   'T.B.'
Langport - Somerton - Castle Cary

The 1822 Greenwood map also shows a 'T.B.' on the B3152 at a cross-roads just north of the Smallway Lane junction at Shepherd's Cross. The Trust maps again differ calling it 'Shepherd's Cross Gate' in 1830 and 'Galhampton Gate' in 1857. The 1830 map shows it on the south-east corner of the crossroads with three gates covering roads west, east and south.

In 1841 'Galhampton Turnpike Gate' was occupied by 'Gate Keeper' Robert Gooden and three children. By 1871 it was referred to as 'Old Turnpike House' as it had been superseded by the 'new' Galhampton Gate (qv) further south.

Galhampton Toll-house
ST 637303
Langport - Somerton - Castle Cary

photo: janet dowding

Built at some time before 1871, the 'new' Galhampton toll-house survives just north of the village at the junction of the main A359 and B3152 to Castle Cary. Built of the local yellow Cary stone, the original doorway has been blocked.

Although not shown on the 1830 or 1857 Trust maps, the 1851 Census shows 2 entries for 'Galhampton Gate', one of which must have been for this 'newer' toll-house. It is therefore not clear when this one took over from the 'old' Galhampton Gate at Shepherd's Cross, half a mile further north. In 1851 Martha Portnell, aged 42, was 'Gate Keeper', living there with a son and daughter and at the same time her husband James, aged 47, was 'Turnpike Gate Keeper' at the old one.

Almsford Toll-house, Castle Cary
(ST 637333)   'T.B.'
Langport - Somerton - Castle Cary

Both Greenwood's 1822 map and the Trust's 1830 map show a turnpike gate at the old junction of the roads into Castle Cary from Shepton Mallet and Somerton. The coming of the railways in about 1856 diverted both roads to rejoin further west at a set of bridges over the railway. The original Shepton Mallet road had cut straight through the present site of Castle Cary station before turning east to its terminus at Ansford Inn.

The Almsford toll-house was thus short-lived, not appearing on the 1857 Trust map, and was superseded by the Shepton Mallet Trust's (surviving) Butwell Gate just north of Ansford bridge at ST 635338 (qv).

Lost Toll-houses West of Castle Cary

Langport - Somerton - Castle Cary

Lovington Toll-house
(ST 592317)   'T.B.'
Langport - Somerton - Castle Cary

Shown on Greenwood's 1822 map as 'T.B.', this site is recorded as 'Lovington Stop Gate' on the 1830 Trust map and as 'Lovington Side Gate' on the 1857 map. It stood just south of the Lydford to Castle Cary road turnpiked under the 1753 Act (present B3153) near the junction with the lane to Sparkford via Lovington village.

In 1871 'Turnpike' was occupied by 'Gate Keeper' Letitia Haskell, a 42 year old widow, and her 11 year old ag.lab son Alfred.

Clanville Toll-house, Castle Cary
(ST 622328) 'T.B.'   'T.Pike'
Langport - Somerton - Castle Cary

Very close to the eastern end of the entire Langport, Somerton & Castle Cary Trust's roads, Clanville toll-house stood just west of Castle Cary, east of the side road junction to Dimmer. Shown on both the 1822 Greenwood map and the first edition 1" OS map, it appeared as 'Clanville Gate' on the Trust's 1857 map and was apparently a two storey building.
In 1861 'Gate Keeper' William Hooper, aged 34, was living there with his wife Hannah and three children. In 1984 it was in a derelict state and was demolished soon after.

Podimore Toll-house
(ST 538254)
Langport - Somerton - Castle Cary

This toll-house stood on the old part of the A372 west of Podimore village (also shown as Podymoor, Poddimore and Puddimore on old maps). This road from Langport to Cobb Door (now Camel Cross) was scheduled to be turnpiked by the 1792 Act but not completed until probably about 1828.

On the 1857 Trust map it is referred to as 'Puddimore Gate'. In 1861 the 'Turnpike Toll House' was occupied by thatcher Joseph Gunter, aged 50, together with his wife Jane and 4 children.

Lydford Toll-house
(ST 566309)   'T.B.'
Langport - Somerton - Castle Cary

There is some confusion as to where the Lydford toll-house actually stood. Greenwood's map shows 'T.B.' near the Lydford-on-Fosse crossroads, where the B3153 crosses the Ilchester Trust's north-south route, both turnpiked in 1753. However the Trust's 1857 map shows 'East Lydford Side Gate' further east on the B3153 at approx ST 568308.
In 1851 'East Lydford Turnpike Gate House' was occupied by 'Turnpike Gate Keeper' Ann Flagg, unmarried and aged 30. However in 1871 'Gate House' is shown on the 'Foss Road' in the parish of West Lydford.

Somerton Toll-house, Cary Bridge
(ST 496290)   'T.B.'   'T.G.'
Langport - Somerton - Castle Cary

Shown as 'T.B.' by Greenwood 1822, Somerton toll-house stood just north of Cary Bridge in the fork between the B3151 to Street and the B3153 to Castle Cary, both roads turnpiked in 1753. Accordingly the two gates adjoining it were known as Street Gate and Butwell Gate.

This old photograph of c.1890 shows it to have had a jettied first floor with two windows, over a ground floor with windows either side of a central doorway. It also had a weighing machine. In 1871 the 'Toll collector' there was Thomas Pollard, aged 44, with his wife Julia and 7 children living with him.

Kingsdon Toll-house
(ST 510270)
Langport - Somerton - Castle Cary

The B3151 from Somerton to the junction at Red Post Cross on the A372 was turnpiked in 1792. 'Kingsdon Gate' appears on the first edition 1" OS map on Kingsdon Hill at the junction of Rocky and Mill Lanes north-west of the village of Kingsdon. It is also shown on both the 1830 and 1857 Trust maps.

The toll-house was burnt down in 1849 but rebuilt within 4 months at the modest cost of £50. In 1851 'Kingsdon Hill Gate' was occupied by James Searle, a 52 year old ag.lab and his wife Ann. In 1871 it was another ag.lab, John Williams and his family, both men presumably taking the tolls as well.

Kingsbury Toll-house
ST 435213
Langport - Somerton - Castle Cary

photo: janet dowding

Situated in the main street through the village of Kingsbury Episcopi, just north-west of the church, this toll-house was shown as No.10 Broad Street in the 1871 Census. It is grade II listed and built of red brick, now whitewashed, with a slate roof and a small canted bay facing the road, a classic Telford type toll-house as might be found in Scotland or west Norfolk.

The road here from Huish Episcopi near Langport south to Broom Bars follows the River Parrett and was turnpiked in 1792. However the toll-house was not built until the 1820's and is shown on the 1857 Trust map.

In 1861 George Grinter aged 34 was the 'Taylor (sic) and Toll Bar Collector' living there with his wife Caroline and 6 children.

West Lambrook Toll-house
(ST 414184)
Langport - Somerton - Castle Cary

The Lambrook Gate is believed to have stood on the road from Kingsbury Episcopi to Shepton Beauchamp, at a junction with the side road to Compton Durville, in the village of West Lambrook. This road was scheduled to be turnpiked in 1792.

Lambrook Gate is included in the 1857 Trust map and in 1851 Samuel Marks aged 59 was 'Gate Keeper', living there with his wife Charlotte. Both were still there in the toll-house in 1871.

Muchelney Toll-house
ST 429250
Langport - Somerton - Castle Cary

photo: janet dowding

Another Telford type toll-house, this time with 'gothick' pointed arched windows, is to be found about a mile south of Langport in the village of Muchelney. Like the Kingsbury example opposite, it too is on the 1792 turnpike road but was built in the 1820's, and is now grade II listed. It is constructed of brick (now whitewashed) with a Welsh slate roof and has a canted bay with a roadside door and two side windows.

It appeared on the 1857 map of toll-houses belonging to the Langport, Somerton & Castle Cary Trust. In 1871 the 'Turnpike toll house' was occupied by 'toll collector' Ann Knapp, a 63 year old widow, living there with her unmarried daughter Sarah. In 1980 it was described as 'now derelict', but has fortunately more recently been rescued.

Park Gate, Westport
(ST 382194)
Langport - Somerton - Castle Cary

On both of the Trust's maps of 1830 and 1857 'Park Gate' is shown at the southern end of the Curry Rivel to Westport Road where it curves and becomes the Ilminster Trust's Puckington Lane. This road was turnpiked in 1753.

It remains unclear whether there was ever a toll-house at this site as no evidence for occupation has so far been found.

Lost Toll-houses Near Langport

Langport - Somerton - Castle Cary

Sutton Toll-house, Long Sutton
(ST 463263)
Langport - Somerton - Castle Cary

The toll-house at West Street, Long Sutton, stood east of Upton Bridge at the crossroads of Long Furlong Lane and Littlefield Lane on the present A372 which was scheduled to be turnpiked under the 1792 Act but may not have been completed until about 1828.

Sutton Gate is shown on the Trust's 1857 map but nothing further is known of it except that in 1851 John Chislett aged 32 was 'Toll Gate Keeper', living there with his wife Charlotte and son William.

Catsgore Toll-house
(ST 511256 / 516254)
Langport - Somerton - Castle Cary

The first edition 1" OS map shows 'Catsgore Gate' at about ST 511256 just east of where Lime Pit Lane joins the main road and south of the present Springfield Farm. It may have been moved as the 1857 Trust map places it at ST 516254 just west of Red Post Cross (south of Kingsdon). Both sites are on the A372, the road scheduled to be turnpiked under the 1792 Act but probably not completed until about 1828.

In 1851 'Catsgore Gate' was occupied by 'Turnpike Gate Keeper' James Noble, aged 68, living there with his wife Mary Ann and daughter Ann.

Westover Gate, Langport
(ST 410265)   'T.B.'
Langport - Somerton - Castle Cary

A 'T.B.' is shown on Greenwood's 1822 map on the present day A378 west of Langport, just west of the junction with the side road to Wick village. This stretch of road from Fivehead to Langport was turnpiked in 1753.

The toll-house once had a weighing machine and in 1861 the 'Toll Collector' was Frederick Hulman aged 43, living there with his wife Maria.

Portfield Gate, Langport
(ST 410267)
Langport - Somerton - Castle Cary

Also shown on the Trust's 1857 map is Portfield Gate, on the side road to Wick village off the Fivehead to Langport 1753 turnpike road.

It is so close to Westover Gate that it could have been a side-gate to the latter, operated by the same toll-collector. There was probably never an actual toll-house there, especially as no evidence has yet been found for any occupation.

Plot Stream Toll-house, Aller
ST 410286
Langport - Somerton - Castle Cary

photo: janet dowding

About two miles north-west of Langport, Plot Stream toll-house stands on the present A372 towards Othery, a road originally authorised to be turnpiked under the 1792 Act.

The red brick toll-house was not built until after the 1824 Act and appears on the Trust's 1830 map. Now grade II listed with considerable extensions added over the years, the original part has the angled front facing the road, with a toll-board recess and the doorway below now replaced by a shaped casement window.

In 1851 the 'Toll Gate Keeper' was George Hallett, aged 51, but Thomas Jenkins, a postman and Post Office messenger, was in residence in 1861 and 1871, together with his wife Elizabeth and daughter Mary Ann.

Beer Toll-house
(ST 404310)
Langport - Somerton - Castle Cary

The A372 from Langport to Weston Zoyland was to have been turnpiked under the 1792 Act, but may not have been completed until c.1828. At the opposite end of Aller parish, a toll-house similar that at Plot Stream was built at Beer Cross, the junction with the side road to Beer village.

On the 1857 Trust map it is referred to as 'Beer Side Gate'. In 1871 'Turnpike Beer Door' was recorded near the blacksmith's cottage and occupied by 'Toll Collectors' Elizabeth Shepherd, aged 57, and her daughter Mary Ann, aged 23, both unmarried.

Moon Cottage, Cossington
ST 357397
No trust

photo: janet dowding

Grade II listed as a toll-house, this late 18th / early 19th Century thatched dwelling is now known as 'Moon Cottage'. Single storey with later additions it has two bays with stone mullioned windows with Y-tracery and pointed heads.

It sits at a junction with a side road to Cossington village, on the main Bath Road (which runs along the Polden ridge used by the Romans, but actually a ridgeway of more ancient origin).

It would not have been much use as a toll-house as it is well set back in its garden. In 1861 it was known as 'Cossington Lodge' and occupied by 55 year old ag.lab Meshack Ames. The Census records give no indication of 'gate keepers' or 'toll collectors' there.

Chedzoy Toll-house
(ST 329353)
Langport - Somerton - Castle Cary

The 1830 Trust book of maps shows Chedzoy Gate immediately east of Langport Bridge and west of Weston Zoyland village on the present A372, 'Weston Zoyland Road' scheduled to be turnpiked under the 1792 Act, but probably not completed until about 1828.

In 1851 the 'Gate Keeper' was Thomas Hunt, aged 29, living there with his wife Martha and baby son George. Chedzoy Gate is also shown on the Trust's 1857 map.

Westhay Toll-house
ST 439432
Ashcott - Wedmore - Rowberrow

photo: janet dowding

About five miles north of Ashcott, Westhay toll-house still stands on the Wedmore Trust's single road northwards across the Somerset Levels to Rowberrow on the Mendip Hills. It stands at the corner of 'Main Road' (B3151) and Westhay Moor Drove in the parish of Meare. It has two side wings with catslide pantile roofs and a projecting canted bay with two casement windows and a blank wall facing the road where the original doorway would have been.

In 1871 the 'Turnpike Gate Keeper' at 'Toll Gate House, Westhay' was Isaac Davis, aged 29, living there with his wife Jane as 'Assistant' and their 5 year old daughter Mary Jane. It is still called 'Turnpike House' on modern maps.

Shapwick Toll-house
(ST 418397)
Ashcott - Wedmore - Rowberrow

The Somerset Historic Environment Record shows a toll-house on Station Road on Shapwick Heath, close to Moorgate Farm and Furze Nidon Copse. It would have been built around 1827 when the Wedmore Trust was set up and probably resembled the three surviving toll-houses of this trust, which had small canted bays.

In 1861 the toll-gate was manned by a lone woman, Sarah Wheeler, aged 60 and unmarried. In 1871 'Toll Gate Cot' was occupied by 'Toll Collector' Jane Isaac, aged 61, and her husband William, an ag.lab.

Lost Toll-houses North of Langport

Langport - Meare (High Ham & Ashcott)

Turbary Toll-house, Buscott
(ST 444385)
Langport - Meare

The High Ham & Ashcott Trust was a very minor and late trust set up in 1826. By this time the north to south routes across the Somerset Levels were better drained, allowing roads to be built, including this Trust's only route running from Pict's Hill, Langport northwards to Meare.

Little is known of the 'Ashcott Turbary Toll House', situated at Buscott, a mile north of Ashcott, except that in 1844 a Trust minute notes that a sum of £68 15s. 7d. was spent on it. In 1871 John Cullen, aged 26, was 'Turnpike Gate Keeper & Ag.Lab.', living there with his wife and family.

Sedgemoor Toll-house, Nythe
(ST 426348)
Langport - Meare

Another High Ham & Ashcott Trust toll-house was 'Sedgemoor Gate' at Nythe hamlet, between Pedwell and Cradle Bridge on King's Sedgemoor Drain. A Trust minute gives details of work done there for £28 3s. 7d., one item being £3 4s. 0d. for lettering the toll-board. Near this gate there was also a toll-bar or chain at the end of Butleigh Drove to restrict access to the turnpike road proper.
In 1871 'Nythe Toll House' was occupied by Frederick Tippetts, aged 32, an 'ag.lab. (carter)' and his 'Gate Keeper' wife Harriett, aged 35, plus seven children. Some masonry in a roadside wall remains of this toll-house.

Other Lost Toll-houses in Ashcott

Beside the two toll-houses above, known to belong to the High Ham & Ashcott Trust, two more toll-houses are said by S.I.A.S. to have been situated in the parish of Ashcott. One is thought to have been at the north end of the present Bradley Lane (ST 439366) and the other at the southern end (ST 439364). This would place them on roads belonging to Bridgwater Trust (A39) and Taunton Trust (A36) respectively. Census records show that Elizabeth Berkly, a widow aged 65, was 'Toll Collector' in 1851 at the first one, and Susanna Simpson, a widow aged 69, was 'Collector of Turnpike Tolls' in 1861 at the one on Taunton Road, Ashcott. The latter may actually be the toll-house said to be near Piper's Inn in Taunton Trust (see page 57).

Less permanent arrangements than toll-houses and gates were chains or bars set across approach roads to restrict access to actual turnpike roads. One such was called 'Heathway Toll Bar' and was situated in the village of Meare at approx. ST 453417 at the northern end of Ashcott Road.

Clewer Toll-house
ST 442510
Ashcott - Wedmore - Rowberrow

photo: janet dowding

On the B3151 about two miles north of Wedmore and a similar distance south of Cheddar, this tiny grade II listed toll-house is rather like the examples at Westhay and Shipham, but without the projecting wings. It is just a canted bay attached to a larger two storey building, which may also have been built by the trust for additional accommodation.

It is thus more of a toll-booth and has a pantiled hipped roof atop whitewashed rubble walls with one remaining 2-light casement window and the original doorway now blocked. In 1871 the 'Toll Collector' was Ellen Williams, aged 36, living there with her husband Benjamin, a Chelsea Pensioner.

Bleadon Toll-house
(ST 34?56?)
Roads around Weston-super-Mare

The 1861 Census has revealed an unexpected 'Turnpike' in the parish of Bleadon, just south of Weston-super-Mare. The toll-house has not survived, but was sited somewhere between 'Hurley Hill' and 'Coal Yard River Ax', both locations unknown.

The main road west of Bleadon from East Brent to Weston-super-Mare was never turnpiked, so this is more likely an off-shoot of the very small Weston-super-Mare & Worle Trust dating from 1840. The 'Toll Gate Keeper' was William Wilson aged 36, living there with his wife Hester and 5 children.

Shipham Toll-house
ST 445577
Ashcott - Wedmore - Rowberrow

photo: janet dowding

Now called 'Turnpike Cottage', this small, single storey, grade II listed toll-house stands at the junction of Broadway with the main B3151 road through the village, turnpiked in 1827. The Wedmore Trust was a small late trust with but four toll-houses along a single road for which all repairs were carried out by the parishes according to the 1840 Parliamentary return.

The toll-house is of whitewashed rubble, with a pantile roof, central chimney stack and has two projecting wings. It has 2-light casement windows, each light with a rounded head, and a door opening to the west. In 1871 'Turnpike House' was occupied by unmarried 'Gate Keeper' Ann Slack, aged 31, living there with her 12 year old son Silvanus.

Bleadney Toll-house
(ST 479454)
Wells - Highbridge & Cheddar

Although the toll-house at Mark is the only survivor from this trust, it seems likely that there were others along this fifteen mile stretch of what is now the B3139. It has been suggested in a local history of Wookey that there was a toll-gate and toll-house at the Panborough end of Bleadney.

To date there is no corroborating evidence for this, as no toll collectors or gate keepers have been found in the Census returns for Bleadney.

Mark Toll-house
ST 379479
Wells - Highbridge & Cheddar

photo: janet dowding

The last of the Somerset trusts to be authorised, the Wells, Highbridge & Cheddar Trust was set up in 1841 and had but two roads to look after. The only surviving toll-house is in the village of Mark towards the western end of the trust's territory. It is almost opposite Mark church, at the junction of Kingsway with Church Street, the main road (B3139) through the village turnpiked in 1841.

The two storey toll-house has a typical angled front and the original doorway is now a window. It has been rendered and given modern windows and a rear extension, but still retains its original slate roof and tall red brick chimney stack. In 1861 the 'Turnpike Toll Collector' there was Humphrey Newman aged 33 and unmarried.

Portway Toll-house, Wells
(ST 535457)
Wells - Highbridge & Cheddar

Another suggested toll-house for this trust is at the eastern extremity of the territory at the end of Portway, Wells. Here the Cheddar road (A371) meets the Wedmore and Highbridge road (B3139).

Census records show that certainly in 1861 there was a 'Keeper of Tolls' in Portway: 51 year old William Smith. Later in 1881, eleven years after the trust ceased operating, there was a 'Turnpike Gate Contractor's widow' still living in Portway: 62 year old Matilda White.

Walton Toll-house
ST 466363
Ashcott - Glastonbury - Wells etc.

photo: janet dowding

It was not until 1806 that the Wells Trust decided to build a toll-house on the corner of Asney Road in Walton, about a mile west of Street. It is on what is now the A39 to Piper's Inn and was erected about 1807/8 at a cost of £145, which included gates to both roads and a 'privy adjoining'. Two years later, the toll-collector was allocated one guinea towards the cost of sinking a well. Unusually semi-detached, the adjoining cottage was also owned and let by the Trustees.

An old photograph shows that the third of the building containing the keeper's window and doorway on the main road side has been demolished for road widening. In 1871 Anna Grey aged 27 was 'Gate Keeper', living there with her husband Archibald and 3 young sons. At the demise of the Trust in 1883, the two cottages were sold to the Marquis of Bath for £70.

Northover Toll-house,
(approx ST 486378) **Glastonbury**
Ashcott - Glastonbury - Wells etc.

Also known as Glastonbury Gate, Northover Gate was one of five initial Wells Trust toll-houses dating from 1753. It stood south of Glastonbury between the Mill Stream and 'Pons Perillous Bridge'. Built for £36, it was to the same design as those at Stoberry, Southover and East Wells: 15 feet square externally with a chimney and thatched roof.

Since road users were using local drove roads to avoid this toll-gate, the Trustees decided in 1783/4 to relocate the gate in Street.

Street Toll-house
ST 486372   'T.G.'   'T.B.'
Ashcott - Glastonbury - Wells etc.

This replacement for Northover Gate is about a quarter mile further south in Glaston Road, Street. It appeared on both the first edition 1" OS map as 'T.G.' and Greenwood's map of 1822 as 'T.B.'.

Built of grey limestone with a plaintile roof, it is unusual for this trust in having an angled front. An 'outer' gate of Wells, certainly there by 1801, it also had a stop-gate across The Mead, opposite the toll-house, to catch drovers trying to avoid tolls.

photo: janet dowding

In 1871 'Street Gate' was occupied by 'Toll Collector' George Dowden, aged 52, living there with his wife Ann and 13 year old stepson Henry. George was still there in 1881. When the Trust was wound up in 1883, the porch was removed, the doorway blocked and the toll-house sold to James Godfrey for £60. The gate was sold separately to Mr. W. Clark for £1 15s. and after being on various sites, was eventually put at the entrance to allotments in Brutache Terrace (ST 485371) where it remains today.

Lost Toll-houses on the Glastonbury Road

Ashcott - Glastonbury - Wells etc.

Coxley Toll-bar
(ST 529437)   'T.B.'
Ashcott - Glastonbury - Wells etc.

About two miles south-west of Wells, the trust erected in 1821 a gate across the lane leading from Coxley to Burcott. This lane emerges onto the main road at the Coxley Pound public house and the publican of the time, Thomas Fulton, was given the added responsibility of collecting tolls from people passing through the gate.

Coxley Toll Bar is shown on Greenwood's 1822 map as 'T.B.' and a toll letting notice of 29 October 1877 included the tolls for 'Coxley Stop Gate'.

Polsham Side-gate
(ST 518428)
Ashcott - Glastonbury - Wells etc.

About a mile further on from Coxley there was another side-gate belonging to the Wells Trust.

This was at Polsham Elm where in February 1823 the trustees "proposed erecting a Toll-gate or Bar across the road leading to Polsham village".

The tolls for this side-gate were not included in the toll letting notice of 29 October 1877, so it either did not survive until then or was dealt with on another occasion.

Hartlake Toll-house
(ST 512409, originally ST 515418)   'T.G.'
Ashcott - Glastonbury - Wells etc.

Shown on the first edition 1" OS map as 'T.G.', the original site of Hartlake Gate (without a toll-house) was on the Wells to Glastonbury road (now A39), turnpiked in 1753. It was just south of Southway at the junction with Lower Crannel Drove, but in 1833 the trust moved it to just south of Hartlake Bridge at the junction with Chasey's Drove and appears to have used an existing building as a toll-house, which was sited rather inconveniently.

In 1873 'lessee of the tolls' Joseph Meek wrote to the trustees that his collector would quit unless a new toll-house was put up. The present (rented) one "was out of sight of the Gate and they cannot get out to the Gate in time and when it rains it comes in on their bed". Repairs and a resiting of the gate followed. In 1881 'Hartlake Turnpike Gate' was occupied by 'Toll Gate Keeper' Joseph Hooper, aged 63, living there with his wife Elizabeth as 'Collector of Tolls' and three children. In 1883 at the demise of the trust the gate was auctioned off for 15s.

Keward Toll-house, Wells
ST 542450
Ashcott - Glastonbury - Wells etc.

photo: janet dowding

Known today as 'The Gate House', this grade II listed toll-house was built in 1842/3 when the gate from Southover was moved there. It stands on the A39 at Keward just south-west of Wells, on the north side of Glastonbury Road and was built on a much grander scale than most others, including a coalhouse, stable and gig house. It was apparently insured for £200 immediately after construction. The original part is of stone with a later rear extension of c.1900 in brick.

In 1871 it was still known as 'Southover Gate' when Joseph Meek, aged 42, was the 'Lessee of tolls', living there with his wife and 9 children. The building was sold to Mr. Sherston in 1883 for £120, when the Wells Highway Board demanded that its bow front should be pulled down.

Southover Toll-house, Wells
(ST 545452)   'T.P.'
Ashcott - Glastonbury - Wells etc.

Southover was one of the five initial toll-houses built by the Wells Trust in 1753 and appeared as 'T.P.' on the first edition 1" OS map. It stood just outside Wells at the end of Southover on the south-western route towards Glastonbury.

In 1753 the site was described as being 'near the Bull Inn below Mill Lane', but when Priory Road was built in the late 1830's, a new site was sought for this important toll-house. In 1842 the gate was moved to Keward and the toll-house demolished, the materials being sold in 1844 for £65.

Tor Hill Toll-house
ST 559455
Ashcott - Glastonbury - Wells etc.

photo: janet dowding

Built soon after the 1764 Act by which the Wells Trust was extended, this grade II listed toll-house on the Shepton Mallet road (A371) guarded entry into Wells from the south-east. Built like Stoberry with a wing towards the road, it is of local stone rubble, with a clay pantiled roof and now has a window in an apparent blocked former doorway. It stands just east of the entrance to a quarry, which once supplied the Trust with stone.

In 1871 'Tor Hill Gate' was occupied by 64 year old 'Gate Keeper' and widow Jane Pound. In 1883 at the demise of the Trust the toll-house 'with gardens, coach house and stables thereto belonging' was sold to Mr. Tudway for £90. It is now called 'Tor Hill Gate Cottage'.

Dulcote Side-gate
(ST 564445)
Ashcott - Glastonbury - Wells etc.

Yet another Wells Trust side-gate was at Dulcote where the trustees in 1821 proposed a "Toll Gate shall be erected across the said Turnpike Road leading from Wells to Shepton Mallet at or near the Cross ways at Dulcott". The road south from Dulcote to Steanbow was once a direct route from Wells into south-east Somerset but was disturnpiked in 1821, and is now a minor road.

In 1851 William Forbes, aged 55, was 'Renter of Tolls' there, and in the toll letting notice of 29 October 1877 tolls for 'Dulcott or Torr Hill Stop Gate' were included.

Stoberry Toll-house, Bristol Hill, Wells
ST 551466
Ashcott - Glastonbury - Wells etc.

photo: janet dowding

Originally built for £30, Stoberry Gate was one of the five initial toll-houses built by the Wells Trust in 1754 and stood on the west side of Bristol Hill (A39) north-east of Wells. Between 1773 and 1802 the trust's only weighing machine was sited there, but in 1832 the old weighing engine house was demolished and two years later the toll-house was altered.

Now of two storeys and known as 'Turnpike Cottage', the grade II listed toll-house is built in stone with ashlar dressings with a Welsh slate roof and a later rear extension.

In 1881 'Candle maker and Gate Keeper' William Walter, aged 48, lived there with his wife Emma. In 1883 the toll-house was sold to Mr. Tudway for £80. The toll-board and a large roadside lamp (p.9) are now in Wells Museum.

East Wells Toll-house
(ST 558462)
Ashcott - Glastonbury - Wells etc.

Yet another of the five initial Wells Trust toll-houses stood a little west of where Hawkers Lane joins the Bath Road, the site known as Horsepool Bridge, later Bath Road Culvert.

In 1871 the 'Toll Gate Keeper' in 'Bath Road Toll House' was David Millington, aged 63, living there with his wife Harriet and 11 year old grandson Alfred. At the demise of the Trust, the toll-house was sold for £10 and later demolished. Until the 1950's a plaque commemorated the site stating 'Here stood the East Wells Turnpike 1753-1883'.

Lost Toll-houses Near Ston Easton

Ashcott - Glastonbury - Wells   *Shepton Mallet*

Worberry Toll-house, Chewton Mendip
(ST 608539)   'T.B.'   'T.P.'
Ashcott - Glastonbury - Wells etc.

In 1790 the Wells Trustees decided to erect a 'Box and Chain' near Horberry (sic) Corner north of Chewton Mendip, on the 1753 turnpike road from Wells to Rush Hill (now A39). By the end of the year a toll-house had been erected at 'Hoarbury Crossways' for £50 by Mr. York of Chewton Mendip. It is shown on an 1820 turnpike plan, on Greenwood's 1822 map and the early 1" OS map.

In 1878 when the Shepton Mallet Trust was abolished, the Wells Trust safeguarded its traffic by setting up a side-bar on the lane south-east from the crossroads to Ston Easton. In 1881 the 'Turnpike Gate Keeper' was James Wheadon, aged 49, living there with his wife Martha. In 1883 the house and garden were sold to Lord Carlingford for £50. A plaque now marks the site.

Ston Easton Toll-house
(ST 623547)   'T.B.'
Roads into Shepton Mallet

'Stone Easton Gate' (sic) is shown on the first edition 1" OS map north of the village of Ston Easton, on the Shepton Mallet to Rush Hill road, turnpiked in 1753. Greenwood's 1822 map shows a 'T.B.' on the west side of the road and the 1840 tithe map also shows a toll-house and gate about one hundred yards south of the modern A37/A39 junction.

In the 1819 auction of tolls Ston Easton Gate was let for £360 10s. 0d., quite a profitable sum compared with other gates. In 1871 'Turnpike House' was occupied by 'Toll Keeper' John Raymond, aged 63, living there with his wife Susan.

Strap Lane Toll-house, Ston Easton
(ST 623522)
Roads into Shepton Mallet

The existence of a toll-house at Strap Lane, also known as Chilcompton Gate, was only established from a 1775 map of the Hippisley estate at Ston Easton. It is shown on the west side of the main road (now A37) from Shepton Mallet north to Rush Hill, turnpiked in 1753.

It has been suggested that the early Strap Lane toll-house was demolished between 1779 and 1840 and replaced by a bar. Certainly a side-gate was erected across Chilcompton Lane / Strap Lane in 1838. Another documentary source shows that in 1865 a proposal for a toll-house and gate at Strap Lane to replace a 'Toll Bar' was only dropped after opposition from a local landowner.

Old Down Toll-houses, Chilcompton
ST 629513 and (ST 634513)   'T.Pike'
Ashcott - Glastonbury - Wells etc.

photo: janet dowding

In 1754 a toll-gate was erected in Broadway, 'near Perry's Coffee House', possibly operated from a sentry box or rented rooms. The first toll-collector was local William Vagg; others in the 1760's were James Boulting, George Beaven and Edward Hodges. In 1767 the gate was resited at a new toll-house to which a stone porch was added in 1768. The 1820 turnpike map places this east of '7 mile stone' i.e. just east of the present Clapton Lane. In 1813 the renter there absconded, leaving his wife to face the music.

In 1834 the Trustees considered at a special meeting the resiting of 'Old Down Gate' a quarter mile nearer Wells to tap the lucrative coal cart traffic emanating from the coal pits in the Nettlebridge valley. Old Down Common had been enclosed and the result was this surviving toll-house built in 1835, controlling the junction with Coalpit Lane. In 1858 the Trustees considered moving the gate back to the old toll-house, which had been let to William Ashman Green in 1836 and survived until its demolition c.1860, when the site was sold to Rev. John Davis. Instead however a bar and wooden toll-house were erected controlling the junction with Clapton Lane.

In 1861 the 'Toll Collector' was John Star aged 43, living there with his wife Ellen and 2 young sons. In 1883 this toll-house was sold to the Rector, Churchwardens and Overseers of Binegar for £40. Now known as 'Turnpike Cottage', it retains its original porch and had similar pointed arched 'Gothick' windows until the 1950's.

Nettlebridge Toll-house
(ST 651488) 'T.P.'
Roads into Shepton Mallet

photo: percy lambert

Also known as Stratton Gate, this former toll-house once stood on the Shepton Mallet to White Post (Chilcompton) road, turnpiked in 1780. Probably built originally in 1783, the proposal in 1800 to sell it for £25 and build a new one on Stratton Common did not happen, so it survived in the north-west angle of the crossroads where the lanes from Benter and Stoke Bottom meet the main road, halfway up the long hill out of Nettlebridge. It had a side-gate and in 1819 the annual tolls were auctioned for £160 2s. 0d.

In 1871 the 'Toll Collector of Gates' William Bennett, aged 70, was there with his wife Ann. In October 1878 'Nettlebridge Turnpike House' was sold to Mansfield Turner of Midsomer Norton for £40. After standing empty and forlorn for some years, it was finally demolished in the interests of public safety in 1962.

Emborough Toll-house
(approx ST 625511)
Roads into Shepton Mallet

According to a history of Emborough, the north-south road through Old Down was turnpiked in 1753 by the newly formed Shepton Mallet Trust, which, according to the 1764 Emborough estate map, erected a turnpike gate for toll collection on the eastern boundary of the parish a few hundred yards south of the Old Down Inn.

Nothing further is known of this site, so it may have been short-lived, possibly superseded by the Binegar toll-house about a mile to the south.

Long Cross Toll-house, Doulting
ST 659451   'T.Pike'
Roads into Shepton Mallet

photo: janet dowding

Carefully positioned where two north to south roads cross a low point on a ridge (along which a Roman road once ran) can be found 'Long Cross Gate, a lonely house at a five pronged road junction on the very top of Mendip ridge'. This simple oblong cottage (now much extended) is built of stone, part rendered, with a tiled roof, and has the date 1790 on the roadside wall. It stands on the Doulting to Long Cross Bottom road, turnpiked in 1765.

In 1819 it was auctioned jointly with 'Chelynch Side Gate' for £200 1s. 0d. In 1861 'Long Cross Turnpike Gate' was occupied by 'Turnpike Gate Keeper' Nancy Kingston, aged 46, her son Frederick and father Israel, both masons. In October 1878 the house and garden were sold to Edmund Joseph Daubeny for £45.

Binegar Toll-house
(approx ST 623495)
Roads into Shepton Mallet

A toll-gate was situated at the foot of Marchant's Hill, Binegar on the 1753 turnpike road from Shepton Mallet northwards to Rush Hill. One document calls it the 'New Turnpike', which seems to imply that the old one was that sold in 1836 to William Ashman Green for £20. The 'new' toll-house stood on the west side of the road near New Lane and Lynch House.

In 1871 'Turnpike House', Binegar, was occupied by 'Toll Gate Keeper' Charles Isaac, aged 40, there with his wife Hannah and 5 children.

Chelynch Toll-house, Doulting
ST 649440
Roads into Shepton Mallet

photo: janet dowding

This small terraced cottage on the road from Doulting to Long Cross Bottom, turnpiked in 1765, was once the Chelynch side-gate, controlling King's Road to the north. It was a rented property out of repair in 1849, when the owner's agent declined to help with its upkeep.

Just discernible in the side wall, and still visible in 1967 but obliterated by later rendering, there was the filled-in outline of a small window used to take the tolls and the holes made by the fixings for the gate hinges. Inside, in the thickness of the wall, was a cupboard for the takings.

In 1861 'Chelynch Turnpike Gate' was occupied by 'Turnpike Gate Keeper' Harriet Witcombe, together with her husband 'Freestone Mason Master' William.

Mendip Road Toll-gate
(ST 622457)   'T.B.'
Roads into Shepton Mallet

Also known as Windsor Hill Toll Bar, Mendip Road Gate stood in the angle of two lanes just off the 'Old Bristol Road' from Shepton Mallet to Rush Hill, turnpiked in 1753. The old route via Warren Farm (ST 621467) was lowered in the 1820's and superseded in 1842 by the present A37 further east.

It was auctioned in 1819 jointly with Downside Gate for £802. Despite being on a superseded road, it remained in operation. The Census returns show in 1851 it was known as 'Side Gate' and in 1871 the 'toll collector' at 'Gate House, Mendip Road' was Mary Haden, aged 21 and unmarried.

Downside Toll-houses, Shepton Mallet
ST 624452 and (ST 624448)   'T.B.'   'T.Pike'
Roads into Shepton Mallet

photo: janet dowding

The original site of Downside toll-house as shown on early maps was about a mile north of Shepton Mallet (at ST 624448), on the west side of the road just past a double road junction. It was on the 1753 turnpike road from Lydford to Rush Hill (and onwards to Bristol) with a branch off to Bath. There was a side-gate at this junction, presumably positioned on the east side of the road at the beginning of Bolters Lane or across what is now Kilver Street Hill going southwards (the latter was ordered to be improved without delay in 1819 for an estimated £50).

Downside gate and side-gate were on the very profitable coal traffic route to Bath. The 1819 auction of tolls quotes a figure of £802 as the profit from the tolls after the expense of collecting them for the previous year. It also had a weighbridge and was let jointly with nearby Mendip Road Gate. The annual Sunday toll quoted for these two gates was £30.

In 1848 'Bolters Lane Side Gate' and 'Lodge House' were set up to cover this junction, operating until at least 1871 when 56 year old widow Sarah Butt was 'Gate Keeper', living there with her 15 year old daughter Emily. In 1848 the main Downside gate was moved about a quarter mile to the north near Downside Inn and this new large toll-house was built on the crest of the hill. In 1871 the 'Toll Collector' was Henry Uzzell, aged 33, living there with his mother Cecilia as his 'Assistant'. In later years this toll-house has also been known as 'Hill View Cottage' and 'Mendip Lodge'.

Chilkwell Street Toll-house, Glastonbury
ST 507384
Roads into Shepton Mallet

photo: janet dowding

Guy's map of 1821 shows the original 1793 toll-house at ST 504386 with gates across Bere Lane and Chilkwell Street. Other gates nearby included one erected illegally by the Wells Trust in 1803 at Bere Lane corner (promptly removed), another 'Beer Lane' toll-house at ST 501385 shown on Guy's map and a toll-bar at Edgarley. The 1844 tithe map shows a toll-house on the south side of the road opposite Tor Lane.

In 1860 the Chilkwell Gates were moved to Tor (now Wellhouse) Lane and by April this new toll-house was completed. It has small side windows facing both ways along the street and now a window in place of the original central doorway. In 1841 the 'Gate Keeper' was John Pike, aged 21, and in October 1878 'Glastonbury Turnpike House' was sold to John Godden for £60.

West Pennard Toll-house
(ST 550387 and ST 556390)
Roads into Shepton Mallet

There were two gates at West Pennard, where the road from North Wootton via Redlake and Whitelake Bridges (ST 550406 and 547403) split before joining the turnpike. This road was reported 'in progress' in 1852 and toll-bars would be needed at both junctions. These were erected in due course, but after the windows were broken in February 1854, iron shutters were fixed. In April 1855 'both houses burnt down and were ordered to be rebuilt in brick or stone'.

In 1871 'Turnpike Gate' was occupied by 'Turnpike Gate Keeper' William Shean, aged 67, living there with his wife Ann.

Kilkenny Toll-house, Ditcheat
ST 596357
Roads into Shepton Mallet

photo: janet dowding

"In 1802-3 there was a firm intention to provide a toll house and gate at the foot of Wraxall Hill, ST 601364, with a side gate across the Ditcheat road. This gate still does not appear in the toll letting for 1810 and it seems likely that the reputed Kilkenny toll house ¼ mile further south was the eventual outcome". (from 'Somerset Roads')

This rectangular building stands south of Wraxall on the A37 Shepton Mallet to Lydford road, turnpiked in 1753. Stone built of two storeys and roofed in slate, it has 'Gothick' arch headed windows, a central window replacing its original doorway. Dated 1853 above the door, as with Pye Hill, there is doubt as to its true status as a toll-house. It is not in 1819 auction of tolls nor recorded on the usual old maps or even the Census returns.

Steanbow Toll-house, Pilton
(ST 575401)   'T.B.'
Roads into Shepton Mallet

At Steanbow Bridge, terminus of the 1753 turnpike road, there was a main toll-gate. A further gate was proposed and probably installed in 1803 across the North Wootton and Wells road. In the 1819 auction of tolls 'Steanbow Gates' were let for £111.

Westwards from Steanbow Bridge the turnpike was extended to Glastonbury in 1780. In 1871 when the Census shows 'Turnpike Gate' next to Steanbow Cottage, the toll-house was occupied by 31 year old 'Gate Keeper' George Hill, living there with his wife Sarah and 3 children.

Pye Hill Toll-house, East Pennard
ST 613373
Roads into Shepton Mallet

photo: janet dowding

This large angular building stands at the crossroads on Pye Hill where side roads to East Pennard and Ditcheat meet the main A37, the road south of Shepton Mallet to Lydford, turnpiked in 1753. The road over Pye Hill was to be diverted in 1778, but the work was not completed until the 1820's.

This site was not mentioned in the 1819 auction of tolls, nor shown on Greenwood's 1822 map. It is therefore assumed to have been built after this, but there is no record of toll-collectors or gate-keepers in the Census returns for 1841-71. Currently called 'The Lodge', it is of 2 storeys, roofed in slate, with pointed arch headed windows and a porch facing the road.

Whitstone Toll-house, Pilton
(ST 601414)   'T.Pike'   'T.B.'
Roads into Shepton Mallet

Pilton's other toll-house was where the present day B3136 (original turnpike road) leaves the A361 (old side road to Beardly Batch) just south-west of Elm Farm. There were two gates and the annual tolls for 'Pilton Gates' were auctioned in 1819 for £71 and the Sunday tolls for £6.

In 1851 the 'Renter of Turnpike Tolls' at Whitstone Gate was William White, aged 61, living there with his wife Mary and daughter Charlotte. In October 1878 'Pilton Turnpike House and Garden' were sold to Edward Seymour Bailey for £45 with the instruction to take down and remove the porch. It is believed that the toll-house was pulled down c.1924.

Butwell Toll-house, Ditcheat
ST 634338
Roads into Shepton Mallet

photo: janet dowding

This grade II listed toll-house stands between Brook House Inn and Ansford Bridge on the A371, turnpiked in 1753. This toll-house and a side-gate existed in 1819, when the annual tolls there were auctioned for £446 5s. 0d. In 1856 this final site for the Butwell Gates superseded the Almsford Gate in Castle Cary, when the coming of the railways altered the turnpike roads in this area.

In 1851 it was occupied by 'Toll Gate Renter' George Roberts, aged 23, and his 'Toll Gate Keeper' sister Ann, aged 18. The slate roofed toll-house has lost its roadside porch, but retains its 'Gothick' windows, one blanked out presumably for the toll-board. It was sold in October 1878, at the demise of the Trust, to Samuel Ashton Pretor for £77 10s. 0d.

> **Lamyatt Toll-house**
> (ST 639356) 'T.Pike'   'T.B.'
> *Roads into Shepton Mallet*
>
> Also known as 'Arthur's Bridge Toll House', this site was where a side road to Bruton, turnpiked under the 1810 Act but abandoned in 1867, joined the Ansford to Shepton Mallet road (now A371), turnpiked in 1753.
>
> According to a notice of June 1819, the annual tolls for 'Lamyat Side Gate' were auctioned for just £32. In 1871 'Lamyatt Turnpike Gate' was occupied by Alfred Hobbs, aged 34, an ag.lab, his wife Mercy and son George. He probably collected tolls as well, but the gate may have ceased to function by this date.

Charlton Toll-house, Shepton Mallet
ST 631431
Roads into Shepton Mallet

photo: janet dowding

Shown by Greenwood in 1822 as 'Charlton Gate', there was a toll-house just east of Shepton Mallet at the cross-roads where the ancient Fosse Way crosses the road towards Frome (now A361). In 1819 the annual tolls were auctioned for £91 5s. 0d. and the Sunday tolls for £6.

On the south side of the road, this was demolished c.1823 and replaced by this small rectangular toll-house on the north side, now grade II listed. Stone built, with 2 large ammonites in the front walls, it has an angled bay with a blocked up doorway and deep overhanging eaves for shelter.

In 1861 the 'Turnpike Gate Keeper' was Tammy Butt, a 45 year old widow with 3 children. In October 1878 'Charlton Turnpike House' was sold to Richard Burt for £52.

Cannard's Grave Toll-house
(ST 628413)   'T.Pike'
Roads into Shepton Mallet

Adjoining 'Turnpike Field', a toll-house stood until about 1912 in the south-east angle of the cross-roads below Whitstone Hill, a mile south of Shepton Mallet. In 1819 'Cannards Grave Gate, and Foss Gate (site unknown) with the Side Gate and Weighbridge' were all let for £486. The Sunday toll for these was £30. In 1851 Francis Roberts, aged 53, was the 'Lessee of Turnpike Tolls', living there with his wife Sarah and 5 children.

Some years ago part of the toll-board from here was discovered in a nearby cottage, serving as a floorboard, but its present whereabouts is unknown.

East Cranmore Toll-house
ST 679442   'T.Pike'
Roads into Shepton Mallet

photo: janet dowding

The original Cranmore Gate was built in 1798 at ST 684441, appearing as 'T.Pike' on early OS maps. When Cranmore Hall was rebuilt and its park enclosed, roads were re-aligned and a new toll-house built at a cost of £100, further west where Slait Hill and Turnpike Lane meet the A361. Robin Atthill in 'Old Mendip' says "It was all that a turnpike cottage should be - neat and Gothick, one up and one down". In the 1960's the till for the takings was found built into the thickness of the wall below a window. In the 1819 auction of tolls 'Cranmere (sic) Gates' were let for £89 3s. 0d.

In 1861 the 'Toll Collector' was John Davis, aged 41, living there with his sister Ellen. In October 1878 'Cranmore Turnpike House and Garden' were sold to Richard Horner Paget of Cranmore Hall for £35.

Dean Side-gate, West Cranmore
(ST 673441)
Roads into Shepton Mallet

In 1820 a toll-gate was to be erected at Dean, West Cranmere (sic) across a lane from the Mendip coal pits onto the Shepton Mallet to Frome road. The exemption for the inhabitants of West Cranmore from paying toll at Dean Gate was amended in 1821 to apply 'only to those ... who are not traders in coal and all passage of coals to be paid for'.

Erection of a toll-house was not considered until 1833 and it was probably never built as the gate continued to appear in the Shepton returns until 1855. 'The lane ... overgrown and rutted, with the naked rock scarred deep by the ... wheels of the coal carts'.

Tadhill Toll-house, Downhead
(ST 681463) 'T.Pike'
Roads into Frome

photo: frome museum

About a mile south-west of Leigh upon Mendip, Tadhill toll-house stood on the still unclassified 'Old Wells Road' turnpiked in 1757. Similar to other Frome Trust toll-houses it had a prominent gabled porch. In 1794 a traveller found Tadhill charges higher than most, describing the tolls as "shameful, especially when road materials are so abundant in the area".

In both 1851 and 1861 the 'Gate Keeper/Toll Collector' was Harriet Season, a widow aged 47 (in 1851), living there with her son and daughter. At the demise of the Trust, it became a labourer's cottage and dame school and was latterly known as 'Cook's House'. Demolished within living memory, only a small part of the wash-house wall remains in the roadside hedge.

Pecking Mill Toll-house,
(ST 640379) 'T.B.' **Evercreech**
Roads into Shepton Mallet

The Pecking Mill toll-house was built in 1793 on the Shepton Mallet to Ansford road (now A371), turnpiked in 1753, at the junction with a side road to Evercreech. At the auction of tolls in 1819, this gate with its side-gate and weighbridge was let jointly with Easton Lane Gate for £247 1s. 0d.

In 1861 'Pecking Mill Toll Gate' was occupied by 'Toll Collector' George Parker, aged 40, his wife Elizabeth and 4 children. In 1887, shortly after the Trust was wound up, the toll-house was sold and demolished, but the 1864 toll-board shown on page 13 was re-discovered near Bruton in the 1960's.

Soho Toll-house
ST 696479　　　'T.Pike'　'T.B.'
Roads into Frome

photo: janet dowding

Gates erected at an earlier site in the village of Soho received unwelcome attention from the Coleford miners who repeatedly threw them down. Two gates were resited at the cross-roads further south where this toll-house stands today. Here just north-east of Leigh on Mendip, the Vobster / Coleford to Little Elm road, turnpiked in 1772 because of coal traffic, meets Whitehole Hill (previously Coal Lane).

In 1851 the 'Turnpike Gate Keeper' was Charles Keyford, aged 28, living there with his wife and family. They were still there in 1861, when he had become 'Labourer on Turnpike Road' and Esther his wife was 'Toll Collector', and continued to live there after the demise of the Trust in 1870.

Easton Lane Toll-house,
(ST 637384)　　　　　　**Evercreech**
Roads into Shepton Mallet

Also known as 'Chain Gate', this toll-house is believed to have stood on the north-west corner of the crossroads where Easton Lane and Leighton Lane meet the Shepton Mallet to Ansford road (now A371), turnpiked in 1753.

The Census returns between 1841 and 1871 all list either Chain Gate or Easton Lane Gate close to Westbrook Farm in the parish of Evercreech. Two older ladies living there alone acted as 'Gate Keeper' and 'Toll Collector' respectively, Mary Stone, aged 60, in 1851 and Matilda Tucker, aged 62, in 1871.

Bull's Bridge Toll-house, West Woodlands
ST 776443 'T.P.'
Roads into Frome

This rather plain looking cottage is the surviving Bull's Bridge toll-house at West Woodlands, south of Frome. Built some time after 1775, it was shown as 'Goose Marsh Gate' on Greenwood's 1822 map and appeared as 'T.P.' on the first edition 1" OS map.

It stands at the junction of the present B3092 (turnpiked in 1772 as the Frome to Maiden Bradley road) and the side road to Tytherington (authorised under the 1772 Act but not completed until 1775).

It has been suggested that the Frome Trust might have had something approaching a standard design because the toll-houses at Tadhill, Wallbridge and East Woodlands appear very similar to this one, each with a small gabled projecting porch, jutting out from the main building with small side windows allowing the gatekeeper to better survey the road and halt the traffic.

In 1861 the 'Toll Collector' was William Fussell, aged 42, living there with his wife Mary and 6 children. He must have been a 'poor relation' since the Fussells were a very well known local family in the Mells / Frome area, owning Fussell's Iron Works.

photo: janet dowding

Milton Clevedon Toll-house
(ST 659378) 'T.G.' 'T.B.'
Roads into Shepton Mallet

The B3081 from Prestleigh on the A371 via Evercreech to Milton Bridge was turnpiked in 1753. Just north-west of Milton Bridge, which belonged to the Bruton Trust, the early 1" OS and Greenwood's 1822 maps show 'T.G.' and 'T.B.' respectively at a minor cross-roads, the eastern road going to Stoney Stratton and the western (now gone) via Albion's Mill back to Evercreech.

In 1819 the tolls for this gate were auctioned for £81 6s. 0d. In 1841 'Milton Turnpike' was solely occupied by 'Gate Keeper' John Bown, aged 55. It was still functioning in 1871, but had been demolished by 1887.

East Woodlands Toll-house
ST 791447 'T.P.'
Roads into Frome

photo: janet dowding

This rather plain looking cottage is the East Woodlands toll-house, close to the Horse & Jockey Inn in the village of East Woodlands. It controlled traffic approaching Blatchbridge from the direction of Longleat (Park and House).

This branch road, turnpiked in 1772, never seems to have achieved much importance, as it was effectively a private drive to Longleat, maintained by the Frome Trust!

The stone built toll-house has a plaintile roof and retains its original porch. Close beside it is a contemporary milestone saying 'Longleat House 2 miles'. The 'Toll Gate Keeper' in 1861 was William Woodland, aged 75, living there with his wife Mary.

Bunn's Lane Toll-house
(ST 781429)
Roads into Frome

About a mile south of West Woodlands the Frome Trust had another gate near Brambles Farm, the early 1" OS map showing a building on the north-west corner of what was a cross-roads there, on the road south to Maiden Bradley (now B3092), turnpiked in 1772.

It was most likely a side-gate as the Census entries for 1851 and 1861 show 'Buns Lane Bar' and 'Bunns Lane Toll Bar' respectively. There was a house there as in 1851 the 'Gate Keeper' was Elizabeth Elliott, aged 31, living there with husband Reuben and 4 children and in 1861 it was occupied by 'Toll-bar Keeper (Greenwich Pensioner)' Joseph Whimpey, aged 76, and his wife Mary.

Critchill Toll-house, Nunney
ST 759472
Roads into Frome

photo: janet dowding

Shown as 'Critchill Gate' on Greenwood's 1822 map, this Frome Trust toll-house is one of five in the parish of Nunney. It stands at the bottom of Gibbet Hill on the road towards Nunney, first turnpiked in 1757, but extended to Nunney Church in 1772.

Built of uncoursed limestone with squared quoins, it has a pantile roof and the date 1860 above what was the original front door (now a window) in the shallow roadside porch. Probably rebuilt at that time it has more recently been greatly enlarged.

'Critchill Toll Gate' was occupied in 1861 by 'Toll Gate Keeper and Chelsea Pensioner' John Sargent, aged 35, there with his wife Susanna and 2 small children.

Lamb's Gate Toll-bar, Berkley
(ST 805485)
Roads into Frome

The 1815 Frome Turnpike Roads map shows a toll-bar at Berkley Cross on the present A3098 (turnpiked in 1757).

It stood on the north arm of the junction on the road that led back to Clink and Fromefield (supposedly only turnpiked in 1831). The 1840 Parliamentary Return of Turnpikes shows 'Lamb's Gate'.

The Census records only ag.labs living there (who may have collected tolls), but no 'collectors' or 'gate keepers', so this may therefore be only a toll-bar or ceased to function very early as such.

Cottles Oak Toll-house, Frome
ST 766482   'T.P.'
Roads into Frome

photo: janet dowding

This house to the west of Frome (once the second largest town in Somerset due to the wool trade) stands in Broadway, on what was the main Wells-Frome-Warminster road, turnpiked in 1757. The first edition 1" OS map shows 'T.P.' and Greenwood's 1822 map calls it 'Cotles Oak Gate', showing it on the south side of the road.

The present house on the north side has the date 1861 above the door and is probably a rebuild. It is of stone with a pantile roof and is said to have an original window looking into the later adjoining property. It would also have had a porch and lamp over the door.

In 1851 the 'Toll Collector (Chelsea Pensioner)' was 41 year old James King, living there with his wife Eliza. Both were still there in 1861.

Spring Gardens Toll-bar, Frome
(ST 773496)   'T.B.'
Roads into Frome

Greenwood's 1822 map shows a 'T.B.' in Spring Gardens, Frome, at the junction of what the 1820 Return calls the main Frome to Buckland road (now Coalash Lane) and Cuckoo Hill, close to Bradford Bridge, turnpiked in 1757.

Nothing further is known of it and most likely there was not a toll-house there, only a toll-bar, as no evidence has been found to date of anyone in residence.

139

Wallbridge Toll-house, Rodden
(ST 787477)   'T.Pike'
Roads into Frome

photo: frome museum

About a mile east of Frome, the 1757 turnpike road branched to Westbury (A3098) and Warminster (A362) and at the foot of 'Styles Hill' there was a toll-house, sometimes known by that name. Its gabled wing and projecting porch are similar to many other Frome toll-houses. Unlike most, it does not appear on Greenwood's 1822 map, but 'T.Pike' is shown on the first edition 1" OS map.

In 1841 'Wallbridge Gate' was occupied by 'Lessee of Tolls' William Forbes, aged 45, with his wife Mira and year old daughter. Living with them was 'Toll Collector' Thomas Portch, aged 15. The toll-house lasted until about 1933 when it was demolished for road widening.

Buckland Dinham Toll-house
(ST 752513)
Buckland Dinham - Radstock etc.

'Old Mendip' states "There is a horrifying glimpse of Buckland Dinham about 1830: here coal was drawn through the turnpike gate in trucks containing from 2 to 12 cwt. by men, women and even children under nine years of age. About 12 tons a day would be conveyed through the village by this agonising sweated labour". The toll-house was apparently "a little low building, hardly more than a shed".

The road from Radstock to Buckland Dinham (A362) was turnpiked in 1768 and the 1871 Census places the toll-gate next to the Bell Inn, at the west end of the village. In 1861 Maria Carver, aged 34, was 'Gate Keeper', living there with her husband George, an ag.lab.

Fromefield Toll-house
(ST 780484)
Roads into Frome

photo: frome museum

Also known as 'North Hill Turnpike', the now lost 'Fromefield Gate' shown in this old photograph was a small cottage with a large lamp above its toll-board and a small side window in the adjoining porch. It stood at the junction of Berkley Road with Fromefield (former A361), at the end of the 1810 Frome Trust road out from the town centre; onwards to Beckington this was controlled by Black Dog Trust.

The short stretch of road east to Clink Cross Ways was first turnpiked in 1812 by Black Dog Trust, but in 1831 Frome Trust took it over from North Hill to Lamb's Gate beyond Clink. In 1844 a traveller saw "an elevation in wood over the Turnpike Gate. It was to ascertain the height of a loaded wagon." In 1861 'Gate Keeper' Mary Gould, aged 25, lived there with her ag.lab husband Henry.

Knobsbury Toll-house,
(ST 707531)   **Kilmersdon**
Buckland Dinham - Radstock etc.

The road south from Writhlington to Babington Corner, not turnpiked until 1830, had a toll-house in Knobsbury Lane. The roads nearby were altered quite a bit around 1835: a cut-off to eliminate a sharp bend was made just north of the toll-house and to the south the east-west turnpike of 1768 through Kilmersdon village was diverted southwards to avoid the very steep Gaganham Hill.
In 1841 'Nobsbury Turnpike Gate' was occupied by 'Gate Keeper' Thomas Gullick, aged 53, and his wife Hannah. Still operating in 1871, it was demolished after the Trust was abolished in 1872.

Spring Road Toll-house, Frome
ST 781487
Roads into Frome

photo: janet dowding

This quite large white painted house is called 'Toll Bar Cottage' and is believed to be the site of the toll-bar erected by the Trust to collect tolls on the short stretch of road called Coffin Spring Lane (now Spring Road) between Welshmill and the Bath road (A361, now B3090) described in the 1831 Act. This short road was actually part of a longer alignment that was never built.

'Coffin Spring Gate' was occupied in 1861 by 45 year old 'Wool Worker' Richard Harvey, his wife Charlotte and 6 children. He may have collected tolls as well or the toll-house had ceased to function as such by this date. Such a large toll-house may be the result of later extension or the adoption of an earlier building for the purpose.

Charlton Toll-house
(ST 679524)   'T.Pike'
Buckland Dinham - Radstock etc.

As well as an entry for nearby Kilmersdon, the 1871 Census contains an entry for the village of Charlton: 'Turnpike Toll House' was occupied by coal dealer Mathew Hughes, aged 56, and his 'Turnpike Toll Collector' wife Ann.

It is possible this came into being when the Kilmersdon one (qv) was moved from the top of the hill to the bottom between 1851 and 1861. The 1840 Parliamentary Return only refers to a 'side bar' here. Its actual position is unknown but could have been at ST 679524 or ST 685521, both junctions on the 1768 turnpike.

Coal Lane Toll-house, Frome
ST 765496   'T.Pike'
Roads into Frome

photo: janet dowding

This surviving toll-house dated 1863 on the west elevation was probably rebuilt. It stands at a cross-roads north of Frome on the Buckland Dinham road, turnpiked in 1757. To the west, the never turnpiked Coal Lane leads to Mells and to the east Coalash Lane, also turnpiked in 1757, leads to north Frome via Welshmill. Greenwood's 1822 map shows 'Coal Lane Gate' there, this gate intercepting traffic from the Radstock coal pits.

The original door has been blocked and replaced by a window but the little side window to observe the traffic remains. In 1851 the 'Turnpike Toll Collector' was James Gane, aged 51, living there with his 'Collector's wife' Elizabeth and two children. The A362 was one of the few Frome Trust roads to become a Main Road under the 1878 Highways Act.

Radstock Toll-house
(ST 695547)   'T.Pike'
Buckland Dinham - Radstock etc.

The first edition 1" OS map shows a 'T.Pike' just east of Radstock on the road to Buckland Dinham, turnpiked in 1768. It was just west of the junction of this road with Mells Lane in the Northfield area of Radstock.

It is not shown on Greenwood's 1822 map nor in the Census entries for 1841-71, so may have been short-lived or possibly abandoned when the road north of Radstock to Pow's Ashes (ST 681563) was disturnpiked in 1830 or earlier.

Kilmersdon Toll-house
ST 695524
Buckland Dinham - Radstock etc.

photo: janet dowding

The original site of Kilmersdon Gate was atop the hill west of the village at ST 690525 where School Lane joins the B3139, turnpiked in 1768. The first edition 1" OS map shows 'T.Pike' here and in 1822 Greenwood's map shows a 'T.B.' The toll-gate was moved to its current position in the village between 1851 and 1861. The surviving grade II listed toll-house is of two storeys with two blank first floor window openings (one maybe for the toll-board) over a broad central gabled stone porch. It has a later single storey extension to the left.

In 1871 'Turnpike Toll House' was occupied by 'Toll Collector' James Woolford, aged 18, and his letter carrier brother Edward, aged 16, both also boot makers. After the demise of the Trust, the toll-house was sold to Rev. Thomas Robert Jolliffe for £105.

Oldford Side-gate
(ST 787503)
Warminster - Bath etc.

According to the 1832 turnpike map there was a 'side gate' at Oldford, in what is now Lullington Lane, just off the main Frome to Beckington road (now B3090), turnpiked in 1752.

There seem to have been road improvements around Oldford junctions (ST 788503) so this side-gate may once have been closer to the main road. It does not appear to have had an actual toll-house as no toll collectors or gate keepers have been found in the Census entries 1841-71.

Tucker's Grave Toll-house, Faulkland
ST 751551   'T.Pike'   'T.B.'
Buckland Dinham - Radstock etc.

photo: janet dowding

Shown on both the early OS and Greenwood's 1822 maps, this toll-house stands at Tucker's Grave cross-roads on what is now the A366, turnpiked in 1768. The road north-west to Stony Littleton, also turnpiked then, seems not to have been a success, being disturnpiked in 1830.

Also possibly known as 'Terry Hill Gate', the small stone built toll-house stands opposite the equally tiny Tucker's Grave Inn at an angle to the cross-roads for better visibility. It had some cement rendering and a pantiled roof and after many years of dilapidation was recently renovated reinstating its original appearance. In 1861 William Kimber, aged 64 and unmarried, was 'Toll Collector' living there with his also unmarried sister Elizabeth.

Rode Toll-gate
(ST 802543)
Warminster - Bath etc.

According to the 1832 turnpike road map, there was a 'Turnpike Gate' at Rode, situated close to the mill stream and almost opposite the side road to Tellisford. It would have been next to the present day Rode Mill.

This road from Woolverton to the A361 near Rode was turnpiked in 1773. However it may only have been short-lived or even just a 'stop gate' or 'side bar' as no toll collectors or gate keepers have been found living there in the Census returns for 1841-71.

Beckington Toll-house
ST 801518
Warminster - Bath etc.

photo: janet dowding

Standing where the road from Frome meets the main Warminster to Bath road, both turnpiked by the Black Dog Trust in 1752, Beckington toll-house is believed to be the left hand part of this pair of attached houses on an L-shaped plan. Now grade II listed and known as No.1 Warminster Road, Beckington, the originally 16th Century building was refronted and remodelled in the 18th Century with two storeys plus attic in the mansard roof and then given a shopfront in the 19th Century, flush with the present pavement.

Unfortunately there are no records of toll collectors or gate keepers there in the Census between 1841 and 1871, so its use as a toll-house remains unconfirmed.

Hinton Abbey Toll-house
(approx ST 771583)
Warminster - Bath etc.

That there was a toll-house at Hinton Charterhouse is without doubt, but it is difficult to pinpoint the exact site. The 1841 Census records 'Hinton Abbey Gate' occupied by 'Toll Collector' Thomas Hobbs, aged 50, living there with his wife Jemima and two daughters. The site is placed between Midford and Hinton Abbey so would seem to be on the original Warminster to Bath turnpike of 1752 (now B3110).

In 1871 'Turnpike House' is placed between 'Lodge' and 'Abbey House' so could be on either the B3110 or the later parallel A36, turnpiked in 1833.

Shawford Toll-house, Woolverton
ST 793535 'T.P.'
Warminster - Bath etc.

photo: janet dowding

Just north of Shawford Bridge, south of Woolverton, grade II listed 'Tollgate Cottage' survives on the A36, originally turnpiked in 1752. Believed to have been built at that time, it has an ashlar front with coursed rubble to the sides and a stone slated roof. The porch and door to the south of the curved front may be original, but the lower level rear wing is probably later.

In 1861 'Shawford Gate House' was occupied by 'Gate Keeper' John Trenchard, aged 57, living there with his 16 year old daughter Fanny. In 1871 he was still 'Toll Gate Keeper', this time with his wife Jane and 17 year old daughter Emma. After the demise of the trust in 1879, the Register of Deeds for that year records the sale of 'Shawford Toll House'.

Bathampton Toll-house
(approx ST 768659)
Warminster - Bath etc.

An 1852 map shows a 'T.P.' at St George's Hill, just east of Bath on the south side of the road from Warminster (now A36). This road followed the River Avon via Bathampton right into Bath, to the east end of Sydney Gardens (ST 759654) and was operated by the Black Dog Trust, known until 1829 as the 'Bath & Warminster' or 'Warminster & Frome', when it took its new name from the inn where meetings were held.

In 1851 the 'Toll Gate Keeper' was William Gale, aged 29, living there with his brother Richard, a butcher. It was still operating in 1871 when John Cross was taking the tolls.

Woolverton Toll-house
ST 792542 'T.B.'
Warminster - Bath etc.

photo: janet dowding

A toll-house survives just north of Woolverton in the angle of the junction between the old Warminster to Bath road (B3110), turnpiked in 1752, and the newer A36 route, turnpiked under the 1833 Act. There is the date '1860' above the roundel in the gable, which may be that of a rebuild, extension or alteration. Known today as 'The Old Schoolhouse', the Woolverton toll-house is built of stone with a slate roof and may have been used for different purposes over the years.

On Greenwood's 1822 map a 'T.B.' is shown further south-east at approx. ST 793540 on the road from Woolverton towards Rode, whilst the 1832 turnpike map shows a 'Side Gate' in a similar position. This site may have ceased to operate once the 1833 road to Bath was built and the new toll-house erected north of the village.

The toll-houses of Woolverton and nearby Shawford seem to have been occupied by various members of the same families. In 1841 the 'Toll Collectoress' at Woolverton was 40 year old Ann Yeoman, whilst at Shawford the 'Gate Keeper' was 43 year old John Yeoman. In 1861 Grace Trenchard was 'Gate Keeper' at Woolverton while in Shawford it was John Trenchard. In 1879 when the trust was wound up, there is no record of the sale of Woolverton toll-house (as there was for Shawford) so it may have been disposed of earlier than then.

Midford Toll-house
ST 762607
Warminster - Bath etc.

photo: janet dowding

Midford toll-house stands on the B3110, old Warminster to Bath road, turnpiked in 1752, and was probably built c.1770 of stone with a tiled roof. The 1840 Midford tithe record shows 'The Turnpike House & Garden' with Josiah Giddings as toll-collector then.

Beside the river in the middle of the village, it divided families there, who would have objected to the over zealous collecting of tolls. On 20 January 1853, in the early hours of the morning, the turnpike gates were wrenched out and stolen and the toll-house lamp and back window shot out. A poster offered a £20 reward for information leading to a conviction but the gates were never recovered.

The toll-gate was still operating in 1871 when 'Toll Collector' Mary Cross, aged 52, was living there with her two daughters.

Bathford Toll-house
(ST 791674)   'T.P.'
Corsham - Batheaston Bridge

The first edition 1" OS map shows a 'T.P.' on the present A4, north of the paper mill on the By Brook, north of Bathford village. 'Bathford T.G.' near Shockerwick is mentioned in 'Paterson's Roads' of 1829, and Mark Searle (1930) says that in 1832 "At the Taunton Assizes, 3 men were found guilty of breaking into the dwelling house of Evans Taylor, who kept the Turnpike-gate at Bathford, and robbing him under threats of £13 and his watch. Sentence of death recorded".

Nothing shows there in the Census returns from 1841 onwards, so this was probably a short-lived gate.

Farleigh Hungerford Toll-house
ST 800575
Trowbridge - Edington etc.

photo: janet dowding

This Wiltshire based Trowbridge Trust had responsibility for some 7 miles of roads in Somerset. This surviving toll-house is grade II listed and stands on the A366, turnpiked in 1768, above the village of Farleigh Hungerford, opposite the public house. Built of stone with a tiled roof, it has a simple stone slab porch, not unlike some Cornish examples.

In 1841 the 'Toll Collector' was Thomas Tarrant, living there with his wife Elizabeth. The Trowbridge Trust was abolished in 1870 and the toll-house was sold off. In 1871 it was already known as 'Farleigh Cottage late Turnpike House' and the route became a Main Road in 1880.

Batheaston Toll-house
(ST 781675)
Roads into Bath

'Batheaston Bar' is mentioned in toll leases of 1818 and 1819 and a 'Turnpike' is shown on Manners 1827 map at the junction of London Road and Bannerdown Road. Mark Searle records that in 1829 "On Sunday night, at 12 o'clock, 4 men, toll keepers of the London (Road) and Batheaston Gates, absconded from their posts, without previous notice, leaving their gates open, and until 11 o'clock on the following day there was no person to take Toll, and the carriages etc passed free".

In 1841 'Batheaston Toll Bar' was occupied by 'Toll Bar Keeper' Hannah Edward, aged 50.

Bradford Road Toll-house, Bathford
ST 788663
Bradford - Bathford Bridge

photo: alan rosevear

The grade II listed remains of Bradford Road toll-house stand on the A363 just south of Bathford village. Believed to have been built in the late 18th Century and altered later, it has rubble stone walls with quoins and a projecting central ashlar section to the older part, with blocked windows and a pedimented door. Now roofless, the remaining walls form a feature in front of a modern bungalow.

In 1841 'Bradford Road Turnpike Gate' was occupied by 'Toll Collector' James Collett, aged 35, his wife Sarah and their 3 children. The 1861 Census places it next to Warleigh Lodge as 'Lime Pit Gate' occupied by 'Toll Collector' Thomas Young, aged 62, his wife Ann and their 9 year old grandson Thomas.

Combe Hill Toll-house, Claverton
(ST 778632)
Roads into Bath

Combe Hill Gate, also known as Brassknocker Gate, once stood where Combe (now Brassknocker) Hill joins the present Claverton Down Road. These two roads are believed to have been turnpiked under the 1757/59 Acts and the site is marked 'Turnpike' on the 1827 Manners map of Bath's turnpike roads. The 1819 notice of toll leases puts it in the parish of Claverton, with a weighing engine and wash-house. It is also mentioned in a notice of toll returns for 1823.

In 1841 'Claverton Combe Hill Gate' was occupied by 'Gate Keeper' Ann Deaves, aged 40, and her 13 year old son Charles.

Bathampton Bridge Toll-house
ST 774670
Bridge Trust

photo: janet dowding

Although not strictly a turnpike toll-house, that at Bathampton Bridge has been in existence since the mid 19th Century. The toll-bridge across the River Avon dates from the 1850's, and was altered in 1870/2, replacing an earlier ford and ferry just below the weir. Thought to have been built for the Bridge Company Turnpike Trust, the house stands on the Batheaston (northern) side in Toll Bridge Road.

Grade II listed, built in stone with dressed quoins, it has a high pitched slate roof, irregularly placed small sash windows in chamfered openings and a prominent gabled stone porch with a toll-board on display. In 1881 the 'Bridge Toll Collector' was widow Mary Box, aged 69, living there with nephew Charles Orchard, aged 21. Tolls are still collected today.

Lansdown Toll-house, Weston
(ST 748660)
Roads into Bath

A 'Turnpike' is shown on Godwin's 1816 'Map of Bath' and Manners 1827 map in Lansdown Road, where it joined Richmond Road, near St. Stephen's Church. The toll-house was on the eastern side of this road, initially turnpiked sometime after 1707 and extended as far as the Grenville Monument in 1757.

It is mentioned as early as 1805 in a toll letting notice and in an 1819 lease of tolls notice 'Lansdown Gate & Bar, Parish of Walcot' is said to have had a wash-house and well-house. In 1841 the 'Gate Keeper' was Mary Horsey, aged 40, living there with her basket maker husband Giles and 2 children.

Swainswick Toll-house, Bath
ST 763673   'T.B.'   'T.Pike'
Cirencester - Bath

photo: janet dowding

Shown as 'Swainswick T.Pike' on the first edition 1" OS map and 'T.B.' on Greenwood's 1822 map, this grade II listed 'Turnpike Cottage' stands on the Old Gloucester Road just north of the village of Lower Swainswick. This part of the A46 is now unclassified but was part of the Gloucestershire based Cirencester & Bath Turnpike which came right down the hill to Lambridge on the London Road east out of Bath. Thought to have been built c.1784, the slate roofed original toll-house has an angled front in ashlar with a blocked in doorway, the rear walls mainly of squared stone with 2-light casement windows. It was extended to the rear in the 20th Century.

In 1861 'Renter of Turnpike Tolls' John Strange, aged 65, lived there alone. In 1871 Charles Casely, aged 44, was 'Toll Gate Keeper'.

Bathwick Toll-house
(ST 755643)
Roads into Bath

On Godwin's 1816 map of Bath there is a 'Turnpike' with toll-house and gates, shown at the bottom of Widcombe Hill. The gates go across the road leading to Bathwick, now the much widened Pulteney Road (A36). The turnpike stands between two 'basons' of the Kennet & Avon canal and close to one of its locks.

In 1823 toll lease notices show 'Bathwick Gate' in operation 'on the road to Bathwick', in the parish of Lyncombe & Widcombe, and that it had a wash-house. It is also mentioned in toll auction notices of 1805 and 1809, and shown on the 1827 Manners turnpike map of Bath.

153

Bailbrook Toll-house, Swainswick
(ST 769668)
Roads into Bath

This 1830 lithograph from Mark Searle's 1930 'Turnpikes and Toll-bars' illustrates 'Bailbrook Turnpike-gate', designed by Edward Davis, a pupil of Sir John Soane, very much in the old master's style. It was a "turnpike toll-house to be erected on the London Road (now A4) near the stone dividing the parishes of Swainswick and Batheaston".

In 1829 "4 men, toll keepers of the London (Road) and Batheaston Gates, absconded from their posts, leaving the gates open....until the following day there was no one to take Toll and the carriages etc. passed free". In 1871 'Tollgate Keeper' James Moon, aged 54, and his wife Eliza occupied 'Turnpike House (London Road)'.

Claverton Street Toll-house
(ST 753643)
Roads into Bath

Godwin's 1816 map of Bath shows a 'Turnpike' with a toll-house and a gate crossing the eastern end of Claverton Street, at the north end of Lyncombe Hill, just east of the present St. Mark's Church. It was also shown as 'Turnpike' on Manners 1827 map. 'Claverton Gate' appears in toll auction notices of 1805 and 1809 and 'Widcombe Gate or Claverton' is shown in 1819 on a lease of tolls, in the parish of Lyncombe & Widcombe with a weighing engine and wash-house. In 1823 'Claverton Gate Bar' is also shown in a return of tolls.

In 1871 'Toll Collector' Henry Tanner, aged 56, lived there with his wife Sarah and his unmarried 30 year old 'Assistant' daughter Rebecca.

Grosvenor Toll-house, Bath
ST 759662
Roads into Bath

This grade II listed building is the Grosvenor Toll House, built in the 1820's and marking the start of the Grosvenor turnpike, the real beginning of the great road to London. This old drawing of 1826 (from Searle, 1930) shows it to have originally been smaller with the same central doorway and two main gates across both ways of the road and a pedestrian gate. In a toll lease dated 10 April 1819 it is called 'London Gate, Parish of Walcot' and described as having a weighing engine & bar, and a brewhouse. It stands in the angle between St. Saviour's Road and London Road (A4). In a report of tolls taken in a typical week of 1823 'London Road Gate' took £63 13s. 5d.

There must have been an earlier building here as 'London Gate' is mentioned in toll auction notices of 1805 and 1809. In 'Paterson's Roads 1829' it is called 'Walcot Turnpike' and is said to be 106¼ miles from London. Now known as 'No. 1, Balustrade', in 1871 it was occupied by William Popjoy, aged 40, a boot & shoe maker. Immediately below London Road, there used to be Grosvenor Suspension Bridge across the River Avon and in 1871 this also had a toll-house and 'Toll bridge keeper': 75 year old Jeremiah Deverill living there with his wife Sarah and 6 boarders.

photo: janet dowding

155

North Parade Bridge Toll-house, Bath
ST 753647
Bridge Trust

photo: janet dowding

According to Pevsner's Architectural Guide for Bath, North Parade Bridge was originally built in 1835 by W. Tierney Clark in "cast iron with rusticated ashlar piers, one enclosing a staircase to the riverside, another formerly a toll collector's residence". The more recent 20th Century bridge is now clad in ashlar but the toll collector's house survives. According to Mark Searle (1930) "The lamp pedestals that separated the Toll-gates were surmounted with carved caps, on which were fixed vases, and on them, were large bronze lamps".

There was a toll-collector living there as early as 1841, his actual accommodation possibly being the rooms with doors and windows surviving today on the level below the bridge facing the river. In 1871 the 'toll collector' was 56 year old widow Elizabeth Cook, living there with her 7 year old nephew Harry Griffith.

Park Farm Toll-house, Bath
(approx ST 743651)
Roads into Bath

Another lost Bath toll-house is indicated by the 1871 Census. Just after an entry for 'Park Farm' there is one for 'Old Toll House' occupied by George Long, a labourer, followed by entries for 'Marlborough Lane'.

'Park Farm House' still exists in Royal Victoria Park so the toll-house could conceivably have been at the corner of Marlborough Lane and Upper Bristol Road at approx. ST 743651.

Halfpenny Bridge Toll-house, Bath
ST 753643
Bridge Trust

photo: janet dowding

This 1862 grade II listed toll-house is situated on Halfpenny Bridge in Bath. Also known as Widcombe Footbridge, there was only one collector who took tolls on the Widcombe side. Originally of a timber bowstring design, the bridge collapsed in 1877 under the weight of the large number of people using it to cross to Beechen Cliff to visit an exhibition. According to Mark Searle many people were thrown into the river and onto the towpath and the proprietors and toll-keeper were found guilty of manslaughter.

The toll-house has a room on each of three levels and is built of limestone ashlar with a slate roof. According to a plaque, the new 1877 bridge has a riveted steel girder and a steel lattice balustrade, built by Westwood Baillie & Co. for the engineer T.E.M. Marsh.

Weston Toll-house, Bath
(ST 73?65?)
Roads into Bath

No accurate site can be found for the 'Toll House' in the Ecclesiastical District of All Saints, Weston, shown in the 1871 Census as occupied by 'Toll Collector' William Brain. The entry was preceded by 'Taylor's Court' and followed by 'Park Terrace', neither of which can be identified.

Since no turnpike road went through Weston village itself, this toll-house was probably sited somewhere along the length of Newbridge Hill or Upper Bristol Road. The latter is suggested by the 1841 Census which records 'Gate Collector' Thomas Mills, aged 45, living there (not to be confused with 'Blue Lodge Gate').

Twerton Toll-house, Bath
(ST 744646)
Roads into Bath

'Bristol Gate', also known as 'Twerton Gate' was a familiar landmark until it was demolished in the mid 20th Century, as shown in this old photograph. It is the single storey building on the left, just east of the Royal Oak public house on the Lower Bristol Road in Twerton, Bath. 'Lower Bristol Gate' and 'Bristol Gate' were mentioned in toll letting notices of 1805 and 1809 respectively. In 1823 a tolls return shows this gate to have taken £54 9s. 7½d. in a typical week.

In 1841, 55 year old Thomas Ogilvie was 'Turnpike Toll Collector', living there with his wife Mary. An 1871 plan for a new toll-house slightly farther east seems not to have been implemented, presumably because of the 1878 demise of the Trust.

Blue Lodge Toll-house, Bath
(ST 737653)
Roads into Bath

Searle (1930) mentions the existence in 1770 of a toll-house on the Upper Bristol Road. In 1823 a return of tolls lists it as 'Blue Lodge Toll Gate' or 'Upper Bristol Road Gate', taking a typical weekly sum of £44 4s. 0d.

It was shown on the Manners 1827 map at the western side of the junction of Weston Lane (now Park Lane) with Upper Bristol Road, opposite Walcot Quarry (now part of Royal Victoria Park). 'Blue Lodge' itself was a short distance north of it in Weston Lane. In 1841 the 'Toll Gate Keeper' was George Kerslake, aged 25, living there alone.

Cross Post Toll-house, Newton St. Loe
(ST 714656) 'T.B.' 'T.Pike'
Roads into Bath

photo: duncan harper

The Old Turnpike, Newton, Bath

The first edition 1" OS map shows 'Cross Post T.Pike' and Greenwood's 1822 map shows 'T.B.' in the angle where two roads north and south of the River Avon join on the south bank three miles west of Bath: Newbridge Hill from Bath via Weston was turnpiked in 1759 and the Lower Bristol Road via Twerton was turnpiked in 1757.

Sometimes known as Newton toll-house, 'Cross-Post Gates' turnpike was mentioned in auction of tolls notices of 1805 and 1809, with two gates and a wash-house, and mentioned again in a tolls return of 1823.

In 1871 'Collector of Turnpike Tolls' Isaac Smith, aged 64, lived there with his wife Mary and two adult children. In more recent times a toll-board discovered in Keynsham and now in Bath Postal Museum, is believed to have originated at Cross Post.

This old photograph shows the toll-house to have been a rectangular building with a canted bay facing the fork in the road. It was built of stone with round arched windows and a slate roof, and was a well known landmark when approaching Bath along the A4 from the west right up until c.1967 when it was demolished to make way for dual carriageway from the fork to the Globe Inn further west.

Red Post Toll-house, Peasedown St. John
ST 698572
Roads into Bath

photo: janet dowding

The Red Post toll-house survives on the A367, turnpiked in 1759, largely along the line of the old Roman Foss Way. It stands at the south end of Peasedown St. John village on the corner of Whitebrook Lane, opposite the Red Post Inn (originally in the parish of Camerton). Built in 1824 of stone with a slate roof, the original part is the single storey building with the projecting canted bay, the rest being later extensions. It now has a concrete tiled roof, modern windows and the original arched doorway has been blocked.

In 1841 and 1851 the 'Toll Collector' was Edward Napps (40 in 1851), living there with his wife Eliza and three children. It was still being operated in 1871 when Jabez Moon, aged 22, was 'Toll Collector'. After the expiration of Bath Trust in 1878 it appears in an old photograph as a bakery, and is now believed to be part of a kennels.

Combe Down Toll-house,
(ST 753623) **Bath**
Roads into Bath

Shown on the 1827 Manners map of Bath's turnpike roads is a 'Turnpike' in Combe Down, on what is now the A3062, turnpiked in 1759. The toll-house stood on the north side of Bradford Road just east of the junction with Fox Hill.

Nothing further is known of it except that in 1851 'Combe Down Gate' was occupied by 'Turnpike Gate Keeper' Charles Dowling, aged 47, living there with his wife Mary and 3 children.

Corston Toll-house
ST 669640
Roads into Bath

photo: janet dowding

This surviving toll-house stands on the Bath to Rush Hill road, turnpiked in 1761 and now the A39. It is about six miles west of Bath adjoining Stantonbury Hill, at the junction with the B3116 to Keynsham. A single storey building with a projecting canted bay, it was built of stone and has a slate roof.

In the 20th Century it became the dwelling/offices of a (Shell?) filling station and acquired its present name of 'The Two-headed Man', the result of an advertisement. Now rendered with modern windows, the original front doorway has been blocked and at present it is unoccupied with an uncertain future. In 1851 the 'Toll Collector' was George Hancock, aged 31, living there with his wife Jane and 3 children.

Kelston Toll-house, Newbridge
(ST 721659)   'T.B.'
Roads into Bath

Greenwood's 1822 map shows 'T.B.' on the south side of Kelston Road, opposite the turn to Weston (now Penn Hill Road). 'Kelston Gate' stood near the 'To Bath 2' milestone on this road, turnpiked in 1757.

It is mentioned as early as 1805 and 1809 in toll letting notices and a toll lease of 1819 shows it had a 'weighing engine and Bar', a wash-house and a 'Block for stopping waggons'. It was also shown on 1827 Manners map showing the location of turnpikes around Bath. In 1861 the 'Toll Collector' was widower Thomas Johnson, aged 61, living there alone.

Marksbury Toll-house
(ST 666625)
Roads into Bath

The old road from Bath to Rush Hill, turnpiked in 1761, went through the village of Marksbury, in the middle of which there was a toll-house as shown on the 1827 map. It was mentioned as far back as 1805 and 1809 in Bath Trust's auction of toll notices, and in a lease of tolls dated 1819 it was recorded as having a weighing engine and wash-house. It was a classic angle fronted two storey building with a pantiled roof and appears to have lost its porch when this photograph was taken in the early 1960's shortly before its demolition.

In 1871 'Marksbury Turnpike' was occupied by John Brookman with his wife and family. Aged 59, 'a landowner and occupier of 52 acres', he presumably also took the tolls.

photo: john ennor

Holloway Toll-house, Bear Flat, Bath
(ST 746638)   'T.P.'
Roads into Bath

The Holloway Gates once stood at the northern junction of the Old Wells Road (now Bloomfield Road) and the new Wells Road (now Wellsway) on the Bear Flat, Bath. Before the latter was built there was only one gate across the road but when the new Wells Road came into being a second gate was needed. In some documents these gates are known as Wells Gate and New Wells Gate. The toll-house stood close to the now lost 'I mile' milestone on the Bear Flat.

On the first edition 1" OS map it appears as 'Holloway T.P. Gate' and in a toll auction of 1805 it is 'Wells Gate'. On the 1827 map of Bath turnpike roads it is simply 'Turnpike'. In a typical week in 1823, it took £97 19s. 8½d. in tolls. In a lease of tolls dated 1819 Holloway gates are shown as having a weighing engine and wash-house. In 1841 'Pike House' was occupied by 'Toll Collector' Henry Scott, aged 40, living there with his wife Elizabeth.

White Cross Toll-house, Hallatrow
ST 629569
Roads into Bath

photo: janet dowding

In 1818 without consulting other trusts in the area, the Bath Trust decided to boost its falling revenues by erecting a new gate at White Cross, Hallatrow (present A37). The toll-house, gate and weighing machine cost nearly £300 and were completed in January 1819.

Strategically placed it collected about £400 annually and remained unpopular with the other trusts, whose tolls it affected. Bath refused to remove the gate across the main road but did eventually remove the side-gate across the Hallatrow road. In 1861 'Labourer and Gate Keeper' Henry Selway was there with his wife Ruth and 6 children. In 1878 at the expiration of the Trust, it was sold for £50 to local landowner William S. Gore-Langton. It has since been doubled in size and is now called 'Turnpike Cottage'.

Burnt House Toll-house, Odd Down
(ST 735617)   'T.B.' 'T.Pike'
Roads into Bath

The southern junction of the old and new Wells Roads had a toll-gate at Burnt House, sometimes known as 'Odd Down Gate'. It appeared on Greenwood's 1822 and the early 1" OS maps and is detailed in toll auction notices of 1805 and 1809, which indicate a wash-house attached.

In 1841 'Burnt House Toll Gate' was occupied by 'Gate Keeper 'Thomas Ogilvie, aged 25, his wife Martha and 4 children. In 1871 it was still operating, occupied by the Hancock family. The Burnt House Inn later occupied this site until a modern block of flats was built there very recently.

Stanton Drew Toll-house
ST 596636
West Harptree - Marksbury etc.

photo: janet dowding

One of the most photographed in Somerset, this tiny grade II listed hexagonal plan toll-house has picturesque 'Gothick' pointed arched windows, a conical thatched roof, tall brick chimney stack and a thatched brick porch. An old photograph shows the last toll-keeper Ann Burridge and her husband (there in 1861 and 1871) next to the then tiled wooden porch, over which a hinged bracket held a leather pouch to receive the toll from drivers of high vehicles.

Just north of Stanton Drew village, it stands on the B3130 Chew Magna to Pensford road, turnpiked in 1793. In 1876 "The Materials of the Toll House and Buildings at Stanton Drew, and the Turnpike-gates, Posts and Rails" were auctioned off, but the toll-house survived.

Stanton Wick Toll-house
(ST 614616)   'T.B.'
West Harptree - Marksbury etc.

The 1840 State of Roads Report places 'Stantonwick Gate' about three miles from the next gate on this road at Wicks Green. It stood on what is now the A368, turnpiked in 1793, at its junction with the side road to Stanton Wick village. The local roads were improved to accommodate coal traffic from Bishop Sutton and Bromley Colliery (just west of this village).

In 1851 'Tollgate Keeper & Laundress' Keziah Harris, aged 29, lived there with her shepherd husband John and their two small children. In August 1876 "The Gates, Posts and Rails of the Turnpike Gates at Stanton Wick, and several Barrows, Rakes etc." were sold off.

Chew Magna Toll-house
(ST 576632)
West Harptree - Marksbury etc.

picture: redcliffe press

As shown in this old picture, Chew Magna toll-house stood in the village, within a stone's throw of the Bear & Swan Inn, at the junction of The Chalks and Tunbridge Road, both roads having gates. It had an angled front, tiled roof, tiled porch and a large lamp.

Chew Magna and Stanton Drew Gates were only 1¼ miles apart, so a reduced rate of toll was levied at these gates and payment at either cleared the other. Double tolls were collected on Sundays.

In 1851 the toll-house was occupied by 54 year old 'Toll Gate Keeper' Charles Weaver, his wife Harriott and one son. At the expiration of the Trust, the materials of the toll-house, gates, posts and rails were auctioned off at the Pelican Inn, Chew Magna on 28 August 1876. It was demolished c.1880.

Wicks Green Toll-house,
(ST 576589)   **Bishop Sutton**
West Harptree - Marksbury etc.

The 1793 turnpike road (now A368) cut a new route through the complex of lanes in the Bishop Sutton area and provided a much improved road for wagons carrying coal from the Bishop Sutton mines to the lead processing works on Mendip. The 1840 State of Roads Report says it was 3 miles from 'Stantonwick' and 2 miles from 'West Harptry', so it most probably stood within Sutton Wick village.

The 1871 Census places it near to Sutton Wick Green Farm, when it was occupied by 21 year old 'Coal Miner' Alfred Gibbs and his 19 year old wife Emma, who presumably also took the tolls. In August 1876 "The Materials of the Toll-house and Buildings at Sutton Weeks, and the Turnpike-gates, Posts, and Rails there" were auctioned off.

Blagdon Toll-house
(ST 501591)
West Harptree - Marksbury etc.

At the west end of Blagdon village a toll-house controlled the junction where the 'Portway' from Bristol, via Winford and Butcombe, crossed the turnpike road, continuing up the hill through Street End towards Charterhouse. The 1842 tithe map shows it (No.303) as a typical small square building set against the wall of Blagdon Court with a short gate across the road from Butcombe and a larger one barring the main road. In 1828 complaints were made that the tolls were 'burdensome' and it was suggested that the tolls be removed for all those living in Blagdon.

In 1861 the 'Turnpike Keeper' was Elizabeth Jenkins, aged 56, who on one occasion was summonsed to the Axbridge petty sessions for charging a Wesleyan minister 6d. carriage toll. He was actually exempt on a Sunday and she was fined one halfpenny and ordered to pay costs.

In 1876 "The Materials of the Toll-house and Buildings at Blagdon and the Turnpike-gates, Posts and Rails there" were auctioned off. The toll-house was demolished for a new entrance to Blagdon Court, probably early in the 20th Century. In 1969 a toll-board was discovered during alterations to a house in Bell Square, Blagdon. It is headed 'West Harptry Turnpike Trust - Blagdon Gate' and shows tolls valid from 25 March 1854. Although split, the painted lettering has survived well and the board is preserved in the house in which it was discovered.

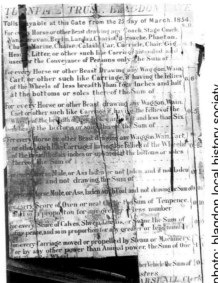

photo: blagdon local history society

West Harptree Toll-house
(approx ST 562568)
West Harptree - Marksbury etc.

The 1871 Census lists 'West Harptry Gate' on the Sutton Road, immediately after 'The Main Street', most likely at the junction at the east end of the village where the main road (A368) heads off north-east away from the Mendip ridge. The 'Toll Collector' then was John White, aged 58, living there with his wife Elizabeth and 5 year old grandson.

In August 1876 "All that TENEMENT or Dwelling-house, Outbuildings, Garden, and Premises situate in the village of West Harptree, and now in the occupation of Mr. William White, and also the TURNPIKE GATES, POSTS,and RAILS there" were auctioned off.

Sidcot Toll-house
ST 426574
Roads into Bristol

photo: janet dowding

Sited between the toll-houses at Cross and Churchill, Sidcot Gate was originally built in the early 1700's. An 1822 notice concerning turnpike houses describes 'New Turnpike House & Gates erected at Sidcot'. Now much extended, all that remains visible today is the projecting angled front, close to the road edge, where a plaque states "The toll for a horse drawn carriage was 4½d. Mail coaches and church-goers exempt".

In 1831 Sidcot and Compton Gates together yielded £788 13s. 4d. and in 1840 it was referred to as 'Sidcott Stop Gate'. In 1861 'Toll Collector' Mary Kerton, aged 60, lived there with her 'sawyer' husband John and their nephew John Thorn, aged 15. After the demise of the Trust in 1867, the toll-house was sold in 1868 to Mary Tanner for £65.

Emborough Toll-house
(approx ST 615511)
West Harptree - Marksbury etc.

In 1876 'The Materials of the Toll-house and Buildings at Emborough, and the Turnpike Gate, Posts & Rails there' were auctioned off by this trust. It probably stood where the southern end of the West Harptree Turnpike (B3114) joined the Wells Trust road (B3139) directly opposite Emborough Pond.

The 1871 Census shows 'Turnpike House' west of the junction with Old Gore Lane, occupied by 'Gate Keeper' James White, aged 37, his wife Amelia and son William. In 1974 part of a toll-board was discovered from an unrecorded toll-house at Emborough.

Churchill Toll-house
(ST 448598)
Roads into Bristol

picture: lynette rice

The Bristol to Bridgwater road (now A38) passes through a gap in the hills just south of Churchill. Remains of the original route, turnpiked in 1749, are visible today and there was a 'T.P.' in the village (ST 445597). A new road was driven past Dolebury Camp to Star in the 1820's with a new toll-house at Churchill cross-roads, of two storeys with a Regency veranda, somewhat similar to Ashton Gate in Bristol.

In 1840 the combined annual tolls for Churchill and Sidcot were reckoned at £1,010. In 1861 the 'Old Turnpike Gate' was occupied by 'Toll Collector' James Giles, aged 58, and his wife Sarah, while 'New Turnpike Gate' was occupied by 'Toll Collector' John Morgan, aged 40, and his wife Mary and family. The later toll-house was demolished in 1961 for visibility at the cross-roads, but the gate and posts survive in nearby Langford.

> **Cross Toll-house,**
> (ST 412547)   **Compton Bishop**
> *Roads into Bristol*
>
> According to a history of Compton Bishop and Cross, on the site of the Cross Memorial Hall there was originally a gate keeper's cottage where the old 1749 coach road turned southwards towards Lower Weare.
>
> An 1822 notice states 'New Turnpike House & Gates erected at Cross'. In 1840 the auction of "The Tolls arising at the Compton Gate …. and at the Side gate, nearly adjoining thereto" were reckoned at £780 p.a. In 1861 'Toll Collector' Henry Carter, aged 30, lived there with his wife Eliza and 3 children.

Chew Stoke Toll-house
ST 560617   'T.P.'
Roads into Bristol

photo: janet dowding

The road south out of Bristol from Bedminster Down came over Dundry Hill and dropped down Limeburn Hill into the Chew valley. In the village of Chew Stoke a 'T.P.' is shown on the first edition 1" OS map. Close to the Stoke Inn, the site is now occupied by 'Turnpike Cottage', which may well be the original toll-house. It has been extended to the left in recent years.

South of the village a section of the old road, turnpiked in 1727, lies drowned under Chew Valley Lake, emerging to climb Harptree Hill on the way to Wells (this latter part was actually disturnpiked in 1819). In 1861 'Toll Gate' was occupied by 'Collector of Tolls' Catherine Dunckley, aged 62, living there with her daughter and niece.

Rownham Toll-house,
(approx ST 564726)   **Long Ashton**
Roads into Bristol

Because of the loss of Bristol Trust's turnpike records, the only remaining evidence for Rownham toll-house is from the Census. It stood on the Bower Ashton to Abbots Leigh road, turnpiked in 1779, which was originally to go all the way to Portishead but never turnpiked beyond Pill.

The 1851 Census places 'Rownham Upper Toll Gate' between Rownham Wood and Rownham Lodge. The 'Toll Keeper' then was Mary Rowles, aged 46, living there with her 'sawyer' husband William and 4 children. William and family were still there in 1861 in 'Rownham Hill Gate'.

Lost Toll-houses South of Bristol

Roads into Bristol

Totterdown Toll-house, Bristol
(ST 699716)   'T.B.'
Roads into Bristol

A toll-house stood at Totterdown on the present A37 Wells Road at the junction with St. John's Lane. Newspapers report in July & August 1749 that it was one of the victims of the Bristol Turnpike Gate riots, when colliers assembled and destroyed the gates.

The road was originally turnpiked under the 1727 Act and both an 1818 map of Bristol's turnpikes and Greenwood's 1822 map show it. In 1851 'Old Turnpike House, Totterdown' was occupied by George Perrott aged 24, an ag.lab.

Knowle Gate Toll-house, Bristol
(approx ST 607707)
Roads into Bristol

According to an 1818 turnpike map of Bristol Trust's roads, there was a toll-house at Knowle on 'The Whitchurch Road' (now A37). It stood in or near the village of Upper Knowle, probably at the junction with the side road to Brislington.

In 1826 an auction of 'The Tolls arising at the Knowle Gate, on the Whitchurch Road' reckoned an annual sum of £660 for this gate. In the year ending March 25 1831, Knowle Gate actually took £755 and in 1840 the annual sum to be auctioned had risen to £730.

Bedminster Toll-house, Bristol
(approx ST 577707)
Roads into Bristol

The Bedminster toll-house is believed to have stood on the present A38, a short distance south of the London Inn on the 'Winford Road'. It also suffered in the 1749 Turnpike Gate riots.

In 1840 'The Tolls arising at the Bedminster Gate, on the Winford Road, and at the Side Gates, nearly adjoining thereto' were reckoned at £1,950. The Census places 'Turnpike House' somewhere in Bedminster between 'Old Bridewell' and 'Parson St.' In 1851 the 'Toll Collector' was John Watts, aged 34, living there with his wife Betsey.

Arno's Vale Toll-house, Bristol
(approx ST 603716)   'T.P.'
Roads into Bristol

The first edition 1" OS map shows a 'T.P.' at Arno's Vale on the Brislington Road, turnpiked under the 1727 Act. The toll-house stood very close to the River Avon, west of the present day cemetery. In 1826 the annual tolls there were valued at £2,405 for auction.

The census of 1861 shows that there were two sites there: 'Old Turnpike Gate' was occupied by 'road labourer' George Russell, aged 37, whilst 'Arnos Vale Turnpike' was occupied by 'Toll Collector' James Lewis, aged 37, living there with his wife Caroline and 9 year old son.

Ashton Gate Toll-house
ST 572717 'T.P.'
Roads into Bristol

photo: janet dowding

A minute of a Bristol Trustees meeting dated 4 March 1823 states that 'the old Ashton Turnpike House' had been sold to James Stokes for £110. The new toll-house, probably built c.1820, is square with a now blocked central doorway in a deep curved central bay. It has a veranda on iron stanchions and a slate roof and stands at the southern end of Coronation Road in the angle with North Street.

A notice of 1822 concerning turnpike houses states "Road raised near new Toll House at Ashton Hill, lowered at the old Ashton Gate". In 1851 'Toll Collector' Richard Stokes, aged 24, lived there with a 16 year old servant. The toll-house closed in 1866 and has been used for a variety of purposes since then but is currently in rather poor condition.

Luckwell Lane Toll-house
(not known)
Roads into Bristol

Also noted in the 1822 notice was a 'New Turnpike House & gates erected at Luckwell Lane', but the actual site of this is not known, although it is probably somewhere near Ashton Gate.

In 1840 the auction of 'The tolls arising at the Ashton Gate, and the Luckwell Lane Gate, on the Ashton Road' gave an annual estimate of income of £1,950 for these gates.

Chelwood Toll-house
ST 625623   'T.B.'   'T.Pike'
Roads into Bristol

photo: polystar

Now much altered and difficult to photograph behind high fences, a toll-house survives at Chelwood on the 'Whitchurch Road', turnpiked under the 1727 Act. It is just south of Whitley Batts, north of the roundabout where the A37 is crossed by the West Harptree to Marksbury road.

It is noted in a local history that in 1826 "By Chelwood Gate twice with a waggon cost 2/6d. The volume of paying carts per day therefore probably wasn't more than about 20". 'Chelwood Gate' took £475 in tolls in the year ending March 25 1831 and in 1840 "The Tolls arising at the Chelwood Gate" were auctioned for £513.

In 1861 the 'Toll Collector' was Robert Gunning, aged 53, living there with his wife Caroline, a tailoress, and his daughter, a waistcoat maker.

Whitchurch Toll-house
(ST 613677)
Roads into Bristol

'Whitchurch Turnpike House' is said to have stood on the Bristol to Wells road (now A37), on the site now occupied by the shop on the corner of Maggs Lane in the village. The 'Whitchurch Road' from Bristol to White Cross (near Hallatrow) was originally turnpiked under the 1727 Act but had parts realigned in 1819.

For the year ending 25 March 1831 Whitchurch Gate apparently took £680 in tolls. In 1840 "The Tolls arising at the Whitchurch Gate and at the Chain or Bar across Ridgway Lane, near the Whitecross Quarry" were auctioned for £635.

Saltford Toll-house
ST 689665   'T.B.'
Roads into Bristol

photo: janet dowding

The Bristol Trust road (now A4) south-eastwards via Brislington to the Globe Inn at Newton St. Loe was turnpiked some time after 1727. An earlier toll-house nearer Saltford (Greenwood in 1822 shows a 'T.B.') had become dilapidated and was replaced c.1829 by this one 100 yards further south-east.

Now grade II listed, it was built in the Greek Revival style, with 2 storeys, stucco walls and a slate roof. The roadside front has a Greek Doric entablature supported by 2 fluted half columns, which until 1910, when the portico was converted into a kitchen, were once free-standing. In 1826 the annual tolls to be auctioned there were reckoned at £2,355. In 1851 Samuel Mockridge, aged 53, and his wife Elizabeth were both toll collectors there.

Other Lost Bristol Toll-houses

Roads into Bristol

Because the Bristol Trust's records have largely been lost, a few other toll-houses appear just as names in a very few documents which mention them south of the River Avon in the old County of Somerset.

For instance in July and August 1749 a newspaper notice included gates at Dundry, Backwell and Nailsea as being victims of the Turnpike Gate Riots in the Bristol area. Their sites remain unknown but apparently a crowd of 400 destroyed the Dundry Turnpike Gate.

5.0 References and Bibliography

Albert, W. 1972 *Turnpike Road System in England 1663-1840* Cambridge
Atthill, R. 1971 *Old Mendip* David & Charles
Belham, P. 1973 *The Making of Frome* Frome Society for Local Study
Bentley, J.B. & Murless, B.J. 2004 *Somerset Roads - The Legacy of the Turnpikes. Phase 1 - Western Somerset. Phase 2 - Eastern Somerset* Somerset Industrial Archaeological Society reprint
Brooke, L. *The Book of Yeovil* Barracuda Books
Buchanan, C.A. & R.A. 1980 *The Industrial Archaeology of Central Southern England* Batsford
Chard History Group 1968 *The Roads, Canals & Railways of Chard*
Clarke, L.A. 2002 *The Minehead United Turnpike Trust* SIAS
Clifford, S. & King, A. (eds) 1993 *Local Distinctiveness* Common Ground
Cole, J. (ed) 1989 *Wanstrow Through the Ages* Postlebury Parish Church
Couzens, P. 1972 *Bruton in Selwood* The Abbey Press, Sherborne
Cruickshank, D. & Wyld, P. 1975 *London: The Art of Georgian Building* Architectural Press
Dewey, H. 1961 *South-West England* British Regional Geology HMSO
Durham, I. & M. 1991 *Chew Magna & the Chew Valley in Old Photographs* Redcliffe Press
Farrington, S.M. 2005 *Wiveliscombe - A History of a Somerset Market Town* Golden Publications
Gosling, G. & Huddy, F. 1993 *Somerton, Ilchester & Langport in Old Photographs* Alan Sutton
Haines, C. 2000 *Marking The Miles A History of English Milestones* Haines
Haynes, R. & Slocombe, I. 2004 *Wiltshire Toll Houses* Hobnob Press
Janes, R. 2003 *Pensford, Publow & Woollard* Biografix
Jordan, M. 1994 *The Story of Compton Bishop & Cross* R.A. & M. Jordan
Legg, R. 2005 *The Book of Wincanton* Halsgrove
Morland, B. 1982 *An introduction to the Infrastructure of the Industrial Revolution in Somerset*
Mogg, E 1829 *Paterson's Roads* London
Mowl, T. & Earnshaw, B. 1985 *Trumpet at a Distant Gate* Waterstone
Parfitt, R. (ed) 2001 *The Book of South Stoke with Midford* Halsgrove
Pawson, E. 1977 *Transport and Economy: The Turnpike Roads of Eighteenth Century Britain* Academic Press
Searle, M. 1930 *Turnpikes and Toll-bars* Hutchinson
Serjeant, W.R. & Penrose, D.G. (eds) 1973 *Suffolk Turnpikes* E Suffolk RO
Smith, P. 1970 *The Turnpike Age* Luton Museum and Art Gallery
Wedlake, A.L. *A History of Watchet* Exmoor Press
Welch, F.B.A. & Crookall, R. 1948 *Bristol and Gloucester District* British Regional Geology HMSO
Windum, A. 1998 *The History of Nunney* Frome Society for Local Study
Wright, G.N. 1992 *Turnpike Roads* Shire

Acknowledgements:

Richard Raynsford:
for use of his Greenwood 1822 maps and bridge photographs

Tim & Ann Jenkinson:
for advice and help on locating 'toll collectors' in the Census

Mike Hallett:
for his comprehensive listing of Somerset Turnpike Acts

Percy Lambert, John Ennor, Duncan Harper, Shirley Melligan, Lynette Rice, Dennis Burry and Castle Cary & Ansford Living History Group:
for use of their toll-house photographs.

Somerset Industrial Archaeological Society:
for various bulletins / journals detailing turnpike gates and toll-houses

Somerset Heritage Centre & Somerset Historic Environment Record

Bath Record Office

Wells & Mendip Museum

Frome Museum

Blake Museum, Bridgwater

Blagdon Local History Society

Ilchester Museum

Of Related Interest

The Toll-houses of Cornwall
Patrick Taylor   2001   £7.95
ISBN 0 902660 29 2   iv+80pp
Federation of Old Cornwall Societies

A comprehensive survey of the toll-houses of Cornwall, dating mainly from the 18th and 19th Centuries.

Illustrated with an extensive gazetteer, this was the first in a series that plans to cover the entire country.

"A useful detailed county study with photographs of high quality"
Industrial Archaeology Review

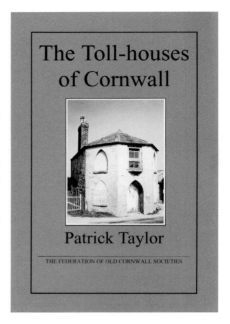

The Toll-houses of South Devon
Tim Jenkinson & Patrick Taylor
Polystar Press   2009   £8.95
ISBN 978 1 907154 01 0   iv+120pp

A comprehensive survey of the toll-houses of South Devon, dating mainly from the 18th and 19th Centuries.

Illustrated with an extensive gazetteer, the first of two volumes covering a large county rich with turnpike remains.

"The book has quality and is attractively presented .... packed with excellent photographs, old and new"
The Milestone Society Newsletter

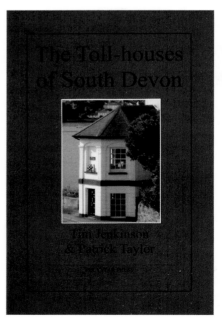